FOSTER'S IRISH ODDITIES

Allen Foster was born in Dublin in 1974, and works as a researcher and writer. He previously wrote a biography of the eccentric American George Francis Train, inspiration for Jules Vernes' classic fictional hero Phileas Fogg. He currently lives on a dairy farm in County Meath and shares fleas with a small dog called Ziggy.

FOSTER'S
IRISH
ODDITIES

a Miscellany of Strange Facts

ALLEN FOSTER

NEW
ISLAND

Foster's Irish Oddities
First published 2006
by New Island
2 Brookside
Dundrum Road
Dublin 14
www.newisland.ie

The author has asserted his moral rights.

ISBN 978 1 905494 40 8

Second impression 2007

British Library Cataloguing in Publication Data. A CIP catalogue record for this book is available from the British Library.

Illustrations by Dougie Ferris
Printed in the UK by CPD (Wales) Ltd, Ebbw Vale.

10 9 8 7 6 5 4 3 2

To my family

INTRODUCTION

Foster's Irish Oddities is a collection of strange Irish trivia. Essentially it is an Irish version of the wonderful *Ripley's Believe It or Not* books that were once extremely popular. I spent countless hours rummaging through old books and newspapers, but it was worth the effort to find the unjustly forgotten, unusual and startling facts that this book preserves.

If you like this book, you will love the *Fortean Times* (www.forteantimes.com, PO Box 2409, London NW5 4NP, UK), a monthly magazine dedicated to the strange and unusual. Peter Somerville-Large's *Irish Eccentrics* and Mary Mulvihill's *Ingenious Ireland* are two other books that will fascinate readers.

Painstaking efforts have been made to ensure that all the bizarre trivia within *Foster's Irish Oddities* are correct. In a book with so many facts, it would be hard to believe that some errors have not been made. If you spot any mistakes or would like to contribute any strange facts, please email them to irishfacts@eircom.net, or send them to the author c/o New Island, 2 Brookside, Dundrum Road, Dundrum, Dublin 14.

Paul Sieveking, Peter Somerville-Large, Mary Mulvihill, Aedamar Corcoran, Deirdre Nolan, Fidelma Slattery, Ronan Gallagher, Thomas Cooney, Dougie Ferris, Ronan Quinlan, Jonathan Williams, Howard Davies, the kind staffs of the National Library of Ireland and NUI, Maynooth Library, and many other unsung heroes deserve credit for their part in this book's creation.

AFTER a lifetime of adventure, famous Irish gambler Thomas 'Buck' Whaley (1766–1800) died in bed from a chill. He once made a bet for £20,000 that he would travel to Jerusalem and return within two years. He won the bet, beginning his journey in September 1788 and returning in June 1789, having travelled 7,000 miles. He passed away at an English coaching inn in Knutsford, Cheshire. His body was placed in a lead coffin and brought to the town's old assembly rooms. Just after the undertakers closed the lid, an Irishman called Robinson appeared and danced a hornpipe on it.

❧

IN 1824, 1,000 British troops were under attack near the West African village of Bonsaso, facing 10,000 Ashanti warriors. Not unduly worried, since they all had rifles, they formed a square and began to slaughter the spear-wielding natives. However, things went badly wrong when the troops broke open the reserve ammunition boxes to reload. Owing to a clerical error, they found the boxes filled with biscuits. The troops were massacred and their leader, Cork man Charles McCarthy, ended up with his skull being used as a drinking cup by the Ashanti chief.

His jawbones were made into drumsticks and his heart was eaten by the Ashanti principal chiefs. The rest of his bones were distributed amongst the warriors as charms to inspire courage. Only McCarthy's skull was recovered by the British.

❧

THE common or viviparous lizard (*Lacerta vivipara*) is Ireland's only native reptile. Shy and seldom seen, it is yellow-brown in colour and at most 20 centimetres long. When it is to been seen, it is usually basking in the sun: the lizard is cold-blooded and, before it can hunt insects, needs to warm its body to 30ºC (in winter it hibernates). It lives in burrows on bogs and sand dunes. The young are born live (hence viviparous) in litters of up to a dozen.

$\backsim$

IRISH cavalry officer Major General Arthur Moore was awarded the Victoria Cross after he led a charge considered to be a 'mission impossible' during a campaign in Persia in February 1857 against 500 infantry drawn up in a square on the battlefield. Military theory generally considered it impossible for cavalry troops to break up a square of infantry who held their position, but Moore's squadron achieved the feat against fixed bayonets and steady enemy fire. A contemporary account said that Moore's horse jumped over the first soldiers as though on a hunting field. The animal fell dead on the bayonets, and Moore's sword was also broken in the fall. He tried to cut his way out of the *mêlée* with the weapon until a mounted trooper following behind rescued him. The squadron rode clear of the disorganised soldiers and then turned back and attacked again with their sabres. Only 20 of the 500 infantrymen escaped.

$\backsim$

DURING the Easter Rising in Dublin in 1916, fighting stopped twice a day to facilitate the feeding of the ducks in St Stephen's Green.

$\backsim$

A gold inscribed ring, lost in 1891, was found in a shipment of tobacco in Belfast 35 years later and was returned to the owner in Springfield, Kentucky. Mr C. C. Bell, a tobacco dealer of Springfield, had been presented with the ring by his wife nearly 70 years previously. In 1925 barrels of Robertson Co. tobacco were shipped from W. H. Simmons and Co. at Springfield to Europe and later were sold to a leaf manufacturer in Ireland. The Bell ring was found in the tobacco. A Mr Cummings, of the Belfast firm, went to Springfield and delivered the ring to Mr Bell's relatives.

꿩

THE longest place name in Ireland is Muckanagh-ederdauhaulia (22 letters), four miles (six kilometres) from Costello in Camus Bay, County Galway. The name means 'soft place between two seas'. The shortest place-name in Ireland is Ta (or Lady's Island) Lough, a sea inlet on the coast of County Wexford. Tievelough, in County Donegal, is also called Ea.

꿩

BOSTON-BASED Irish merchant Captain Daniel Malcolm was a vocal patriot who sold tea and smuggled wine into port. He died just before the Battle of Bunker Hill in 1769 and asked to be buried 'in a stone grave 10 feet deep' to be safe from British bullets. He hated British taxation policies so much that he had his opposition noted on his gravestone. That gravestone, in the Copp's Hill Burial Ground in the North End of Boston, to this day bears the marks of bullets fired by British soldiers who singled out Malcolm's grave and used it for target practice.

꿩

A letter to a former Athboy resident magistrate turned up in Dublin in late April 1991 – still undelivered after 105 years! Postal staff found the postcard addressed to Major Traill, R.M., Heathstown House, Athboy, County Meath, while working on an iron cast letterbox set in the wall of Greene's Bookshop, Clare Street, Dublin. The writer, whose name is unclear, was seeking to order eight dozen eggs daily, or every alternate day if a daily delivery was not possible.

❧

IN the late 1700s, wandering Irish adventurer Thomas Legge from Donaghdee, County Down travelled the Indian subcontinent as a mercenary for hire. He later developed an interest in Indian alchemy and divination and ended his days as a *fakir*, living naked in an empty tomb in the deserts of Rajasthan outside Jaipur.

❧

SOME time around Christmas 1974 a young married woman entered a maternity home in Trim, County Meath in preparation for the birth of her third child. Her medical and nursing attendants were puzzled by a lump on the head of the baby in her womb. Their puzzlement changed to astonishment when the baby was delivered. Its head was 'crowned' with the cap of a Guinness stout bottle! How it got there remains a mystery, heightened by the proud mother's comment: 'I must have swallowed it.'

❧

PADDY the pigeon from Carnlough, County Antrim was decorated for being the first bird to fly back to England with news of the D-Day landings in

Normandy. The citation recorded that the bird returned with the news in just under five hours. Paddy the pigeon is the only animal from the island of Ireland to have won one of 53 so-called Dickin medals awarded in Britain since 1914 as the animal version of the Victoria Cross, granted for conspicuous bravery in wartime.

꿍

FOR more than 30 years, legendary Irish adventurer John Howard Taylor (c. 1904–69) was a professional big game hunter in Africa and was often out of touch with civilisation for as long as three or four years at a time. Taylor said that he did not know of World War II until some of his men brought back provisions from a remote trading post wrapped in old newspapers – only then did he learn the rest of the world was wracked by war!

꿍

THE tallest twins (identical) ever recorded were the Knipe brothers (b. 1761) of Magherafelt, County Derry, who measured 7 ft 2 in (218,4 cm).

꿍

POLICEMEN in Dublin on the night of 9 May 1867 took shelter from an onslaught of nuts or berries that fell from the sky 'in great quantities and with great force' during a 'tremendous rainfall'. The berries were described as being 'in the form of a very small orange, about half an inch in diameter, black in colour, and, when cut across, seem as if made of some hard dark brown wood. They also possess a slight aromatic odour.' According to one observer, the objects were 'simply hazelnuts, preserved in a bog for centuries'. How they had come to fall from the sky was not explained.

⌁

A monkey appears on the Fitzgerald coat of arms in tribute to the family pet, which rescued the infant 1st Earl of Kildare from a fire at Kilkea Castle, County Kildare, in the 14th century.

⌁

CATHERINE Anne Gilmore was delivered by Caesarean section three months prematurely in July 1976. Her mother had been shot in the Ardoyne district of Belfast and a bullet had lodged in her baby's back. It was removed and the child was released from hospital eight months later.

⌁

ACCORDING to the *Guinness Book of Records 1991*, the world's oldest cow and most prolific breeder was Big Bertha, who lived on the farm of Jerome O'Leary near Kenmare, County Kerry. She died on 30 December 1993, three months short of her 50th birthday. Big Bertha was reputed to have had 39 calves, and two daughters, aged 35 and 30, were still on the farm at the time of her death. In her lifetime she was a celebrity and made numerous public appearances, raising large sums for charity. After her death an all-night wake was held in O'Neill's pub in Bertha's local village, Blackwater, County Kerry. Her owner had the rare Droimeann cow stuffed and he continued to tour with her to fundraise for charity.

⌁

TULLAMORE-born writer Elliott Warburton died in a fire on the steamer *Amazon* on 4 January 1852. He had written a novel called *Darien, or the Merchant Prince*, which described such a disaster. His book appeared posthumously.

఼

BARON Münchhausen, traveller and liar, hero of the fantastic novel *The Travels and Adventures of Baron Münchhausen*, was the creation of Rudolf Erich Raspe (1737–94), who died and is buried in Killarney, County Kerry.

఼

IRELAND is the only country in the world that has a musical instrument – the harp – as its national symbol.

఼

THERE are many verified cases of homing animals which have made incredible journeys over great distances across unknown territory towards their home. Some of these animals (usually dogs or cats) travelled thousands of miles to reach their owners. One Irish case on record concerns a cat called Pidge. In July 1948 John J. Crawford of Hewetson School, near Clane, County Kildare, dispatched a small kitten to a friend in Castleblayney, County Monaghan. The kitten was safely packed in a wooden box and travelled by rail via Dublin to its new home. It was such a tiny thing that its new owner called it Midge. For nearly 18 months the tomcat enjoyed a comfortable lifestyle in his new home, growing so large that his owners thought it best to change his name to Pidge because Midge was now clearly unsuitable. All was well until his owners had to move house. Unfortunately, they could not bring Pidge with them, but a new home was found for him with neighbours. Despite being well looked after, Pidge became unsettled and restless in his new abode. He was often seen patrolling his old home, and according to one source became 'embroiled with predatory males, in the less reputable areas of the town'. All was not well on the home front either. Relations with his new master's cat, Rinty, were strained if not non-existent. A few months later matters came to a head when Pidge got involved in a ferocious fight with a neighbouring tomcat and then disappeared. Two weeks later Pidge turned up at his birthplace – Hewetson School – the place he had left 18 months previously as a tiny kitten. Castleblayney is about 74 miles from Clane by road. What unexplained homing instinct enabled Pidge to traverse unknown countryside and find his way 'home' inside a fortnight? John Crawford went to some lengths to establish that the cat which arrived on his doorstep on 1 February 1950 and lay exhausted in his kitchen for several days was the missing Pidge. He checked and rechecked every conceivable clue to his identity, from his characteristi-cally splayed forefeet to his pronounced partiality for dry toast, and was convinced, as was his owner of 18 months, that the cat was indeed Pidge.

⌁

IN January 1994, the *Irish Independent* reported an unusual attack on an elderly couple in Dublin. Three men forced their way into the home of William Cruise (84) and his wife May (85) and stole £168. Thinking quickly, Mrs Cruise locked the door of the bedroom in which the raiders had bundled her and her husband, and managed to climb out a window and raise the alarm. Police described as 'bizarre' the fact that the gang leader was confined to a wheelchair.

≪

GERRY Condron, a butcher from Sligo, was driving towards Ballyshannon, County Donegal, in November 1998 when he saw a flash of light overhead and then smoke coming from a field. Going to investigate, he found a tiny corpse. A Bundoran garda told him it was 'probably a rabbit'. A Belfast laboratory carried out tests and marked the specimen 'alien embryo'.

≪

IN July 1995 Seán Gale, aged 33, was stopped for erratic driving outside Clonmel, County Tipperary. He was found to be steering with a pair of pliers. 'The steering wheel came off when we were visiting the mother-in-law,' he told gardaí.

≪

A low-flying swan left two cows dead and more than 200 houses without electricity on 14 January 2002 when it brought down power cables near Castlebellingham, County Louth. The bird died instantly.

≪

IN late May 2004, fishery experts were baffled by the death of hundreds of eels in a small lake on the island of Inishbofin, County Galway, particularly because oxygen levels were not seriously depleted. Dead eels were discovered along an 820 ft (250 m) stretch of shoreline of Lough Bofin, since large numbers of eels had travelled overland in a bid to escape from the lake.

~§

IN preparation for the World Monopoly Championships held in Toronto in October 2000, Ireland's Nigerian-born Monopoly champion, Ekumdayo Badmus, changed his surname to make it sound more 'Irish'. His new name? O'Badmus. He also brought two squares of turf to the competition – to ensure that he would always have a piece of Ireland beneath his feet.

~§

NOVELIST Bill Granger's first thriller concerns an IRA plot to blow up the yacht of a British lord and cousin of the Queen while he is sailing in the Irish Sea. *The November Man* was published as a paperback less than three weeks before IRA bombers assassinated Lord Mount-batten on his yacht off the Sligo coast in 1979. In the thriller, the American hero foils the plot at the last moment.

~§

IN February 1980 Irishman Eddie McAlea went into a Liverpool jewellers wearing a stocking mask, pointed a revolver at three men and warned them, 'This is a stick up. Get down.' They didn't bother because they saw a red plastic stopper in the muzzle and knew the gun was a toy. After a scuffle, McAlea escaped, ripping off the mask as he fled. The jeweller recognised him, for only the day before Eddie had sold him his own watch. He was quickly caught and subsequently jailed for 30 months.

※

AS dawn broke, Michael Martin, 24, was pulling his boat up to the bank of misty Lough Ree on the opening day of the duck-shooting season in September 1987. His Labrador, Lindy, stepped on the trigger of his single-barrelled shotgun and shot her master in the leg.

※

IN February 1984 the £3,000 mare Russell's Touch had unseated its trainer, David Kiely, while training on the shore at Dungarvan, County Waterford, before dashing into the foam and heading out to sea. Kiely spent the next two hours trying to raise a rescue boat. Eventually the horse was spotted by a returning trawler. A rope was passed through the horse's stirrups and the noble but daft beast was ignominiously towed ashore. It recovered after a few days.

※

ONLY one man has ever dared steal the Crown Jewels of England. He was Meath-born daredevil adventurer Colonel Thomas Blood and he did it in broad daylight on 9 May 1671. If it had not been for a twist of fate, Blood would have got away with it. Unlike many other thieves of the time, Blood escaped the hangman's clutches. King Charles II was so impressed with his daring that he pardoned Blood and rewarded him with a large annuity.

※

THE world record for being on the run was broken by jail-breaker John Hannan from Ireland in November 2001. Police were half-hoping he would give himself up for the sake of getting his name into the *Guinness Book of Records*, but weren't holding their breath. Hannan had avoided capture for an amazing 46 years, just beating the 45 years and 11 months of American Leonard Frisco, who was turned in by his son after an argument. Hannan was sentenced to 21 months in Verne Prison in Dorset, having been convicted of car theft and assaulting police officers in 1955. He escaped after just 31 days. He is still on the run. 'We are no longer actively searching for John Patrick Hannan, but we'd still love to find him, even after all these years – there's a small matter of some unfinished business,' a Dorset police spokesman said. 'If he does learn we are still looking for him, we would love to hear from him, even if he just drops us a line to let us know he's still around.'

JOHN St John Long, a handsome young Irish artist, started offering cures for tuberculosis in 1826. By the 19th century, incurable 'consumption' had become the most dreaded disease. Long earned over £10,000 a year for rubbing a secret salve into his patients' skins. He was especially successful with women, but did not save them. He was twice prosecuted for manslaughter. Once he was acquitted; the second time he was fined £250. Happily for medicine, he died when he was only 36 – from tuberculosis!

A Spanish tourist got more than she bargained for while on a short holiday in Dublin some years ago. She was admiring Christ Church cathedral when two young Dubliners with a baby in a buggy struck up a conversation with her. They chatted amiably, then the pair suddenly snatched the tourist's handbag and ran off – leaving their baby behind. At first the woman thought it was a practical joke. What self-respecting criminal would leave their baby behind at the scene of a crime? When they did not return with her handbag and claim the baby, the woman informed gardaí at a nearby station. Several hours later the child's mother gave herself up at the station and asked for her baby. This story was deservedly included in a book about the world's dumbest criminals.

IN her declining years, once famous actress and beauty Mrs Patrick Campbell was nursed through a spell of illness in 1940 by her close friend, Irish actress Sarah Allgood. When she recovered, Mrs Campbell gave her friend a beautiful watercolour of a heron as a keepsake. Afterwards they went their separate ways: Mrs Campbell to France and Sarah Allgood to Hollywood, California. Sarah's first dream in her new home in America was of Mrs Campbell. In an unusually vivid dream her friend appeared and spoke to her. 'Have you found my gift from the grave?' she asked. 'Look behind the picture.' Sarah was puzzled by the dream, because she had no reason to believe that her friend was not still alive. But she checked behind the painting and found a hidden treasure. It was a caricature of Mrs Campbell by the famous writer and caricaturist Sir Max Beerhom, worth about $2,000. Sarah Allgood later learned that her friend had died on the day of her strange dream.

❧

ONE of the strangest court cases took place in Derry on 11 December 1926 when a legless ex-soldier was prosecuted for cycling on the footpath at Ballymacgroarty, near Derry. Henry Doherty, a veteran of World War I, had lost both his legs in that conflict. To aid his mobility, the Ministry of Pensions had given him a hand-propelled tricycle. One day the machine broke down. Doherty's brother-in-law, William Doherty, came to the rescue of the stranded invalid and attached one end of a rope to the tricycle and the other to his own bicycle and started to tow him home. An overzealous constable named Junk came across the two men travelling on the pavement, one pulling the other by a rope which was attached to the two vehicles, and cold-heartedly issued them with a traffic offence summons. The case was struck out.

❧

IN the early 1980s, researchers at Trinity College, Dublin wanted to do some work that needed woodworms – plump ones. The only ones that were available were too thin, so Dr Seán Thompson, leader of the team, fed them on dog biscuits. Within a month they had grown to 20 times the size of an average woodworm.

❧

THE famous song 'It's a Long, Long Way to Tipperary' was written by two friends, Jack Judge and Harry J. Williams, in 1912 as the result of a bet. A group of actors challenged them to write a song and perform it the same day. So they sat down in a pub and did just that. Connemara had originally been chosen after much discussion, but Judge switched the title to Tipperary. Williams was furious at not being consulted, but this last-minute change made the song. It became popular among troops as a marching song in World War I and quickly became world famous, making a fortune for its creators.

⤜

THE Wonderful Barn of Leixlip, County Kildare is 73 ft high, with an outside circular stairway of 94 steps, and was built during the famine of 1743 to provide employment for the needy.

⤜

IN 1999 a group of 40 Romanians disguised them-selves as a choir and sent an application, complete with fake awards and testimonials and a tape of the choir singing (in reality it was another choir), to take part in the Sligo International Choral Festival. They were booked for the opening night. The Irish consul in Bucharest gave the group their visas. When the 'choir' arrived in Dublin, they vanished. Some successfully applied for asylum, others are still unaccounted for.

⌘

IN November 1999 Queen Maeve, a duck belonging to Willie and Kitty Costello of Belclare, County Galway, laid an egg which earned it a place in the *Guinness Book of Records*. Extensive research confirmed that Queen Maeve had laid the world's largest duck egg. Almost as big as an ostrich egg, it measures over 8 inches in diameter and weighs 227 grams. When the outer shell was broken, another egg was found inside, perfectly formed and intact. A researcher with Guinness World Records, Ms Rasila Kuntwala, said that this in itself was very unusual.

⌘

WHILE Elizabeth Thompson was travelling to Spain in the 18th century to be reunited with her future husband, Barbary pirates intercepted the ship and took the young Irish girl captive, later selling her at a slave market in the Moroccan capital, Fez. The beautiful Cork woman was sold to representatives of Sultan Sidi Mohammed and she became part of the imperial harem. The ruler was captivated by the Irishwoman and made her his Empress. Their eldest son later became Emperor, while Elizabeth lived out her days in the luxurious palace at Marrakech.

⌘

IN 1752 the Church of Ireland Bishop of Raphoe, Philip Twysten, was shot dead while carrying out a highway robbery. By day he devoted himself to God, by night he became an enthusiastic highwayman. The bishop was shot on Hounslow Heath near London by one of his intended victims. The story was covered up, except for a cryptic reference in the *Gentleman's Magazine*, which commented on the fact that the bishop had been mysteriously taken ill on Hounslow Heath and had died of an 'inflammation of the bowels'.

❧

IF you went to see the world's shortest play, you would hardly have time to sit down before it was time to go home again. *Breath*, by Samuel Beckett, lasts just 35 seconds. *Breath* does away with such theatrical conventions as dialogue, plot or actors. The play's stage directions run to only 120 words. The curtain rises on a stage strewn with rubbish, and the only 'action' consists of lighting effects and a soundtrack that starts with the cry of a newborn child, followed by a 10-second breath in, a 10-second breath out, and ends with the cry of a dying person. Beckett wrote the play in 1969, as a contribution to Kenneth Tynan's controversial revue *Oh! Calcutta*. But Tynan altered Beckett's script without telling him. Beckett was so annoyed that he called Tynan a 'liar' and a 'cheat'. What was it that made him so furious? Beckett discovered that Tynan had staged the play using actors. Whether or not he was also upset by the fact that all the actors were naked is another matter. The play was first staged in March 1970.

❧

EIGHTEENTH-century Irish adventurer Beauchamp Bagenal went on a wild Grand Tour of Europe in the 1750s. According to diarist Jonah Barrington, he 'fought a prince, jilted a princess, intoxicated the Doge of Venice, carried off a Duchess from Madrid, scaled the walls of a convent in Lisbon, [and] concluded his exploits with a duel at Paris.' The jilted princess, Charlotte of Mecklenburgh-Strelitz, consoled herself by marrying George III.

A will made by a Belfast woman in 1911 was locked away in a drawer for 13 years. When the drawer was opened after her death, there was nothing left. Rats had eaten the will, except for a few remaining scraps. With Irish enterprise, however, a copy was patched up out of the shreds and the memory of witnesses, and this attested copy was eventually admitted to probate in Belfast on 27 February 1925.

IRISH Guards Officer Lieutenant Charlie Williams survived falling 3,500 feet from an aircraft after his parachute failed to open properly during a training exercise on 25 October 2004. Williams, aged 25, was saved by a corrugated iron roof he smashed through at 120 mph. It broke the army officer's fall as he landed in a shanty town in Kenya. Instead of being killed outright, he escaped with three cracked vertebrae and a dislocated finger.

GEORGE Bernard Shaw left a notorious will which became a 20th-century *cause célèbre*. When his will was heard in March 1951, people were astonished to learn that Shaw had directed that his estate be used to investigate the possibility of substituting an alphabet of at least 40 letters for the existing one of 26. Six years of legal battles later, a judge finally ruled that the alphabet clause was invalid, and that the estate pass to the residuary heirs under the will. After a vigorous campaign by the Shaw Society, a compromise was reached at the end of 1957, with the result that enough money (£500) was put aside to carry out Shaw's alphabet investigation. As his will stipulated, a competition was held in 1958 to create a new writing system for English. Seventy-two-year-old Kingsley Read's system was chosen as the winner out of the 467 entries and was adopted as the Shavian Alphabet. The trust charged with developing the new alphabet was able to afford to publish only one book: a version of Shaw's play *Androcles and the Lion*, in a bi-alphabetic edition with both conventional and Shavian spellings (Penguin Books, London, 1962).

IN his pioneering medical work *Observationes Medicae*, Nicholas Tulp, the Dutch doctor portrayed by Rembrandt in *The Anatomy Lesson*, describes a feral youth captured in Ireland in 1672. The 16-year-old boy had lived with a herd of wild sheep since early childhood – presumably he had been orphaned. The nimble youth evaded capture for some time, but eventually hunters trapped him with a net. He was hardy and healthy despite his rough lifestyle and diet. He displayed many attributes common to feral children: a refusal to change his diet (from grass and hay), the ability to endure extremes of temperature and constant attempts to escape back to his 'family'. Eventually he settled down and became comfortable among humans, but he never quite fit in. Bizarrely, he bleated like a sheep and never learned to talk. He was brought to Amsterdam, where Dr Tulp was able to observe him first hand. The Irish sheep-boy, Tulp wrote, 'had acquired a sort of ovine nature. He was rapid in body, nimble of foot, of fierce countenance, firm flesh, scorched skin, rigid limbs, with retreating and depressed forehead, but convex and knotty occiput, rude, rash, ignorant of fear, and destitute of all softness.'

⁓

IN 1976 the European Economic Community pointed out to the Irish government that it had not yet implemented the agreed sex equality legislation. The government immediately advertised for an equal pay enforcement officer. The advertisement offered different salary scales for men and women!

⁓

THE most protracted yodel on record is that of Errol Bird for 10 hours 15 minutes in Lisburn on 6 October 1979.

⁓

A 1974 dinner dance for the Belfast branch of Alcoholics Anonymous must rank amongst one of the least successful meetings of any AA branch. It ended in a cloakroom brawl after £385 had been spent at the bar. The manager of the hotel the event was held at said the trouble was not so much caused by the AA members: 'It was their friends.'

❧

BEAUTIFUL Irish actress Charlotte Walpole (1758–1836) entertained London theatregoers, married into the British aristocracy and lived a live of bliss. During the French Revolution she became a real-life Pimpernel, in the same mould as the fictional Scarlet Pimpernel. Driven by the need to rescue her friend, the French Queen, Marie Antoinette, and her son, the Dauphin, Charlotte risked death every day as she cleverly disguised herself as a man in soldier's and sailor's outfits to avoid capture. She arranged the most daring rescue plans, only to fail because Marie Antoinette refused to be rescued unless her son, the heir to the French throne, was rescued first.

❧

IN 1968, Mike Meaney from Ballyporeen, County Tipperary, was voluntarily buried alive in a coffin underneath Butty Sugrue's public house in Kilburn, north London, for a total of 61 days.

❧

THERE are rival claims for the sighting of the last great auk, the northern hemisphere's equivalent of the penguin. Most say that the last was killed off the coast of Iceland on 4 June 1844, but others say a great auk was killed on the Saltee Islands off the coast of Wexford by fishermen in 1845.

❧

IN June 1994, Seán O'Malley, 27, from Waterford, hit serious trouble when he tried to flout a nudity ban on a Corsican beach. He was pounced on by two burly locals, who painted him bright red from head to toe.

※

IN 1738, Henry Barry, fourth Lord Santry, was tried, found guilty and sentenced to death for the murder of a pot-boy at the Black Swan Inn in Palmerstown, Dublin. After a day spent drinking in the public house, Barry had stabbed to death the unfortunate pot-boy, Laughlin Murphy. Lord Santry was a member of a wealthy and influential family but all the money and connections failed to secure him a pardon. When everything else had failed, his uncle, Sir Compton Domville, came up with a cunning plan to save his life. The river Dodder, which was Dublin's sole source of water, flowed through Domville's estate in Templeogue. Sir Charles simply threatened to cut off the city's water supply by diverting the river if his nephew's death sentence was carried out. The threat was effective and Lord Santry was saved from the gallows on the understanding that he leave the country and forfeit his rank and estates. His escape was arranged by connivance, and he fled abroad. He spent many years travelling throughout Europe until his death in 1751. Compton Domville succeeded to his nephew's title and estates. Even in death, Barry remained an exile. Although there is a memorial to the wicked peer in a graveyard in Santry, he died in Italy and was buried there.

※

IN 1811, 70-year-old Corkonian John Purcell earned a knighthood for killing four burglars with a carving knife. How an old man, alone and unaided, fearlessly faced a room of armed raiders is an extraordinary story. At about one o'clock on the night of 11 March, Mr Purcell heard a noise outside his dining room window. This room adjoined the room in which he slept, but the door between was nailed up and a sideboard had been placed against it. Hearing the dining room windows being forced in, Purcell jumped out of bed, determined to resist this unlawful invasion of his property, but he had no arms. How was he going to defend himself? Suddenly remembering that he had taken his supper in his bedroom, he groped round in the dark for the carving knife, which, fortunately for him, his servant had forgotten to remove. Having found it, he stood ready beside the intervening door, and not a moment too soon, for the robbers were moving away the furniture, and soon the door burst open. The first man to enter was stabbed. The next man met the same fate. The intruders fired a gun into the darkness of Purcell's bedroom, but it missed him. He killed another man who tried to attack. The thieves now launched a combined attack. As soon as they got near enough, Purcell struck right and left with his knife. Purcell wrestled with an attacker and was hit on the head, but he managed to kill the man. By now the carving knife was bent and useless. Purcell took a sword out of the dead man's hand and successfully fought the others off with it. He made such good use of the weapon that the robbers hastily retreated, dragging their dead and wounded with them. This brave deed did not go unrewarded. On 12 July of the same year the Lord Lieutenant of Ireland, the Duke of Richmond, knighted the venerable old man. Afterwards he became known by the honorific nickname 'The Knight of the Knife'.

᠅

AN unnamed Ulster Loyalist was shot by an under-cover soldier in Belfast on March 1993. He escaped death when the bullet shattered a brass Chubb key in his jacket pocket, deflecting it away from his body.

᠅

RETIRED businessman Klaus Schmidt, 64, was on a Lufthansa flight from Dublin to Frankfurt in May 1998 when he suffered serious heart problems and had difficulty breathing at 11,000 feet. The chief steward asked if there was a doctor on board, and was met with 40 raised arms from the entire German delegation returning from an international medical seminar in Ireland. Many were carrying newly developed heart drugs in their hand luggage. A professor from Heidelberg loos-ened Mr Schmidt's collar, while a specialist in micro-scopic surgery gave him an injection. Within minutes, the colour returned to Herr Schmidt's cheeks and he was breathing more easily. He was able to walk from the plane when it landed, with some help. 'I was lucky to choose the right flight,' he told a stewardess. 'I'd been thinking of flying back the next day and then changed my mind.'

᠅

A shoe once worn by St Bridget, one of Ireland's three greatest saints, is enshrined in the National Museum of

Ireland, Dublin in a silver casket. She became a nun at age 13 in a ceremony during which she was also consecrated bishop – the first Christian woman to be so ordained. Contemporary accounts chronicle her miraculous deeds and emphasise her work in spreading Christianity throughout Ireland.

❧

AFTER spending over two decades looking for his long-lost sister, Philip Yeomans was pleasantly surprised to find that she lived down the road from him in Paignton, Devon. Born in Wexford, he was brought up by his aunt after his father died and his mother suffered a breakdown. The aunt died in 1975 and he spent the next 22 years and £5,000 travelling 20,000 miles in search of relatives. In early 1997, he placed an appeal notice on the ITV Teletext service. Finally his girlfriend, Judith Woodward, mentioned his epic search in passing to Mary Sammons, 52, a fellow care assistant at a Paignton nursing home, who realised that she was Philip's sister. Mrs Sammons, a mother of six, said: 'We met and got on like a house on fire.'

❧

AFTER his death, the famous Clonmel-born writer Laurence Sterne's body was stolen from Bayswater Road Cemetery in London by body-snatchers and sold to the Professor of Anatomy at Cambridge University for dissection at one of his classes. While his remains were actually being dissected, he was identified. The lecturer had already sawn the top off the skull, but orders were immediately given for the demonstration to be concluded and the body to be reinterred. In 1969 the graveyard was sold for development as flats. The Laurence Sterne Trust learned of this and immediately sought permission to exhume his body for reburial at Coxwold, Yorkshire, where he had lived. The grave contained five skulls and several bones, but one skull had the top sawn off, evidence of the body-snatching. Further proof was provided when the measurements matched those of a bust of the author, and so the remains were taken to Coxwold and reburied. Sterne now has two tombstones at Coxwold: a white one with black letters which is full of errors, while a second one now corrects those.

❧

THE luck of the Irish held good for John Delany, aged 56, in August 1979. He was walking past a building site in Birmingham when a huge concrete coping stone, weighing at least a hundredweight, fell two floors and landed squarely on his unprotected head. Horrified police, ambulance men and doctors expected him to die from terrible brain damage. The next day he sat up in his hospital bed and remarked: 'I've got a bit of a headache. That's all.' Delany also had a fractured skull and a cut requiring 17 stitches, but he swiftly recovered.

❧

ONE of Ireland's unsung heroes is an inventor named John Francis Byrne. In 1918 the Dubliner invented a unique unbreakable code using a homemade device called a 'Chaocipher', which was little more than a cigar box and a few bits of string and odds and ends. He tried without success to sell it to various governments, but none was interested. In America he demonstrated it to the head cryptanalysts of various government and military bodies and telephone companies, but they all rejected it. When Byrne published his autobiography, *Silent Years*, in 1953, he included a description of his invention and a lengthy message in Chaocipher code. He bet £5,000 or the total royalties earned in the book's first three months of publication that no one could solve the code. It remains unbroken to this day. There are said to be only a handful of people trusted with the secret knowledge of Byrne's cipher. Byrne was a close friend of James Joyce. In his novel *A Portrait of the Artist as a Young Man,* Joyce modelled his character Cranly after him.

≪

THE Chapel of St Oran on the island of Iona in the Hebrides holds the tombs of four Kings of Ireland, 48 Kings of Scotland, eight Kings of Norway and four Kings of France.

≪

THE world's record for riveting is 11,209 in nine hours by J. Moir at the Workman Clark Ltd shipyard, Belfast in June 1918. His peak hour was his seventh with 1,409, an average of nearly 23.5 rivets per minute.

≪

IN October 2002, Lisa Landau, a champion horsewoman, incredibly survived 34 hours buried in a ditch after her car plunged off a road near Ashford, County Wicklow. Lisa was trapped in her upturned, and almost submerged, car for nearly two days, just feet away from a busy road. Miraculously, she survived by breathing through an air pocket she managed to find near a brake pedal. Her rescue occurred by chance when a passerby neighbour, Chaim Factor, noticed bark missing from a tree and went to investigate. He discovered the car and called gardaí.

~

THE oldest recorded living wild bird is a 55-year-old Manx shearwater, which has made its home in County Down. The venerable bird was first ringed in the Copeland Islands off Donaghadee, County Down in July 1953, when it was at least five years old, and again in the same place in 2003. It has been estimated that the bird has clocked up some five million miles during its lifetime.

~

ON 15 August 1920, all the religious statues and pictures in the homes of Thomas Dwan and his sister-in-law, Mrs Maher, in Templemore, County Tipperary began to bleed simultaneously. News of the miracle spread throughout the country, and the initial trickle of pilgrims increased to a torrent. Special excursion trains from Dublin to Templemore were organised, and the Thomas Cook Travel Agency inquired if the local inns could accommodate 2,000 pilgrims. Pilgrims came from as far away as the United States, South Africa, Japan and India. A sea of tents, dubbed Pilgrimsville, surrounded Templemore on all sides. In the earth floor of a room belonging to a lodger of Mrs Maher's, a hollow the size of a teacup miraculously filled with water from an unknown source. Pilgrims took gallons of it away with them, but the water was always replenished. At first people were admitted to the two houses in groups of 50, for five minutes at a time. Later, the statues were displayed in the windows and processions of pilgrims trooped past the houses. By night they carried torches. It was estimated that by the time the statues had stopped bleeding, roughly a month after they had begun, close to one million people had visited Templemore, County Tipperary.

❧

HAVING already given birth to 19 children, Emily, Duchess of Leinster (1731–1814), eloped with their tutor, William Ogilvie, after the Duke's death and had another two offspring with him!

❧

KILDARE man Henry John Beresford Clements (1869–1940) earned the unusual reputation of being the world's most acknowledged expert in the specialised field of 'armorial book-binding'. This was a 14th-century practice, greatly developed in subsequent centuries, whereby the family arms of private individuals were placed on book covers. Henry's collection, bequeathed to the Victoria & Albert Museum in London after his death, is the largest of its kind in the world.

❧

THE longest working life recorded in Britain or Ireland was that of Susan O'Hagan (1802–1909), who was in domestic service with three generations of the Hall family of Lisburn, Northern Ireland for 97 years, from the age of 10 to light duties at 107.

❧

THE deepest underwater escape was made by Roger Chapman and Roger Mallinson from a depth of 1,575 ft (480 m) off the coast of Ireland in 1973. Their vessel, *Pisces III*, had sunk and they remained trapped for 76 hours before escaping.

᭟

THE following example of a remarkable coincidence, sent to Arthur Koestler after the publication of his book *The Roots of Coincidence* in 1973, may be too good to be true. The author of the letter, Anthony S. Clancy of Dublin, writes: 'I was born on the seventh day of the week, seventh day of the month, seventh month of the year, seventh year of the century. I was the seventh child of a seventh child, and I have seven brothers; that makes seven sevens. On my 27th birthday, at a race meeting, when I looked at the race-card to pick a winner in the seventh race, the horse numbered seven was called Seventh Heaven, with a handicap of seven stone. The odds were seven to one. I put seven shillings on this horse. It finished seventh.'

᭟

IRELAND'S oldest pillar post box was erected in 1857. The hexagonal roof pillar box is located in Kent Railway Station, Glanmire, Cork.

᭟

A promising young Irish jockey who fell from his horse during a jump race in 1956 died from his injuries 48 years later. Cornelius Kenneally, of Prestbury near Cheltenham, died from chronic renal failure on 25 June 2004. Deputy Cotswold coroner Sally Scanlon said that the condition which killed him was directly linked to his riding accident in 1956. As a 16-year-old, Cornelius was riding in a race at Chepstow when his horse failed a jump, rolled over and fell onto him, leaving him paralysed from the waist down.

᪨

WELL past their sell-by date, Ireland's oldest biscuits were discovered at a ringfort site at Lisleagh, County Cork. The 1,300-year-old snacks are the oldest prepared foodstuff ever found in Ireland. Scientists who have prepared a fresh version using the ancient ingredients say that the oatmeal biscuit is crisp and nutty, and not as sweet as modern brands. Duchy Originals oatcakes, the brand made on the Prince of Wales's estates, are thought to be their closest equivalent. The pieces of biscuit were uncovered some years previously and were initially thought to be pottery. Their true composition and importance were discovered only in 2004, after being scanned with an electron microscope and undergoing chemical investigation.

᪨

ANN Borodell (1615–1712) of Cork, after her marriage to George Denison of Stonington, Connecticut, received from her father as a dowry her weight in gold – exactly 90 pounds.

᪨

IN 1912, 'When Irish Eyes are Smiling' was written by George Graff and Chauncey Olcott, two canny American songwriters, who, as far as is known, never set foot in Ireland.

᪨

CHRISTIAN Cavanagh (1667–1739) was the daughter of a prosperous Dublin brewer. In 1683 she disguised herself as a man to follow her husband, Richard Welsh, into the army. Described as a rough diamond, strong and self-reliant, her exploits against the French in Holland became legendary and it was not until she was wounded at the Battle of Ramillies in 1706 that her sex was revealed. Following the death of Richard Welsh at the Battle of Malplaquet in 1709, Christian was to marry again, twice – once to a grenadier, Hugh Jones, and later to another soldier named Davies, before spending her last years running a public house in London, where her fame attracted many customers. She died in 1739 after a period in Chelsea Hospital and was buried with full military honours.

❧

THE guillotine was used by the Irish nearly 500 years before it was adopted by the French. An old print portrays an execution of a gentleman named Murcod Ballagh using one near Merton, County Galway on 1 April 1307.

PLUCKY 90-year-old Bridget M. McCormack, of Largan, Carrick-on-Shannon, County Leitrim, who hobbled about with the aid of a stick, managed to catch a marauding fox single-handed. Entering her poultry house late at night on 29 December 1945, she saw a fox, carrying a turkey, trying to escape through a ventilation opening with its victim. Mrs McCormack watched in amazement as the fox got stuck and the lucky turkey escaped. Acting quickly, she caught the fox by its tail and dragged it to the kitchen door, which she jammed on the brush. Her shouts brought her son, who killed the animal with a hay-fork. As a reward for her actions, Mrs McCormack received eight shillings, a bounty given for every fox killed.

⤚

THE Congressional Record of 17 April 1934 contains the remarkable story of an Irishwoman who had continuously suffered from asthma for 101 years, before she was finally cured of it at the age of 112. Dubliner Belle Rhynes emigrated to the United States in 1822, aged 11. She began to suffer from asthma as soon as she arrived there.

⤚

MISS Letitia Overend of Airfield, Dundrum, County Dublin, who died in September 1977, was the longest continuous owner of a Rolls Royce car in the world. Her cherished car was a 1927 model.

⤚

THE only civilian who ever commanded a United States man-of-war was Robert B. Forbes (1804–89). He was placed in command of the 800-ton *U.S.S. Jamestown*, which transported food to Ireland during the famine of 1845–47.

≈

PENELOPE Smith of County Cork was so proud of landing the Prince of Capua as her husband that she married the Italian royal four times in 1836. To one of the ceremonies she invited 13 suitors whom she had rejected.

≈

CORK-born Edward Hincks (1792–1866) was one of the most learned Egyptologists and Assyriologists of his age. He was so bright at languages that he was made a fellow of Trinity College, Dublin before he was 21.

≈

A 1922 edition of *Scientific Monthly* included a report on a Colonel Townsend of Dublin, who could 'die or expire when he pleased, and yet…by an effort he could come back to life again.' A well-known physician, Dr Cheyne, recounted: 'I found his pulse sink gradually, till at last I could not feel any by the most exact and nice touch.' Cheyne's observations were verified by two colleagues, and he records: 'Dr Baynard could not feel the least motion in the breast nor Dr Skrine perceive the least soil on the bright mirror he held to his mouth…We began to conclude he had carried out the experiment too far, and at last we were satisfied he was actually dead.' But the colonel came round the next morning, there for all to see, a very extreme case of anomalous body control.

≈

ON 7 April 1984, a lightning strike did more than ruin Tony Cosgrave's round of golf while playing at Baltray, near Dublin. A bolt of lightning struck him, causing serious injury, resulting in emergency medical treatment and hospitalisation for the professional golfer. Thankfully Cosgrave recovered and resumed his career. Surgeons discovered that his bowel had been perforated by an explosion of gases ignited by the lightning, which had probably entered his body through a brass belt buckle.

⁓

THE man appeared to be slightly drunk when he entered the bank in Macroom, County Cork, in October 1992. He shouted, 'This is a stickup!' and claimed that he was armed with a weapon hidden under a coat folded over his arm. Unfortunately for him the coat slipped, revealing his arm but no weapon, at which point he announced, 'It's an invisible gun.' He was laughed out of the bank.

⁓

BY the age of 14, William Rowan Hamilton (1805–65) was familiar with the rudiments of 13 different languages: Hebrew, Latin, Greek, French, Italian, Spanish, German, Syriac, Arabic, Sanskrit, Hindustani, Malay and Persian. When he was only seven years old he was able to carry on a conversation in nine languages.

⁓

A large fireball was seen over the Irish Sea on 21 October 1926. At about 9.30 a.m. an observer in Ardglass, County Down spotted a dense black cloud over the Isle of Man. Under it suddenly appeared a large ball of fire. Immediately after there was a violent report of thunder, but no rain fell. The sun then became visible and the cloud faded away.

⋘

GRANDMOTHER Mary Ward was having her highlights done at the Cut and Dye salon in Ballygraigue, County Tipperary in early April 2005 when she had a vision of the late Pope, John Paul II. 'The view appeared on my lap on the black gown,' she said. 'He was smiling. I then asked one of the girls if she could see anything, and she said, "Oh my God, it's the Pope."' Mrs Ward set up a shrine at home, with the gown as a centrepiece.

⋘

ERNEST Shackleton (1874–1922) from Kilkea, County Kildare is famous as one of the greatest polar explorers. In recent years a cottage industry of books and documentaries based on his exploits has emerged. Most of this renewed interest in the Irish explorer centres on his now legendary Antarctic expedition of 1914–16. The expedition was a failure, but because of the astonishing feat of survival that followed under Shackleton's inspired leadership, it is remembered as a triumph over adversity. In August 1914, Shackleton and a 27-man crew set out to be the first to cross Antarctica. In January 1915, the *Endurance* became stuck fast in ice close to the continent. For nearly nine months it drifted helplessly, before finally being crushed, leaving the men stranded 200 miles from land and over 1,000 miles away from the nearest living souls. There was no possibility of anyone coming to rescue them: if they were to survive, they would have to depend on their own resources and determination to overcome the incredible odds against them. They camped out on drifting ice floe until April 1916. Once the ice started to break up, they took to the two lifeboats they had managed to save and made a hazardous seven-day voyage to desolate Elephant Island, where they set up camp. With five other men, Shackleton set out in one of the small lifeboats in a near suicidal attempt to get help. They endured a 17-day journey across 800 miles of the world's roughest seas before reaching South Georgia Island, where a whaling station was located. Shackleton and two other men made a desperate 36-hour trek over treacherous glaciers to reach the station. After several failed attempts, he managed to rescue the remaining men on Elephant Island on 30 August 1916. Amazingly, not a single life was lost throughout the ordeal.

'BLACK rains and black snows – rains as black as a deluge of ink – jet black snowflakes.' Such a rain fell in Ireland on 14 May 1849, described in the *Annals of Scientific Discovery* (1850) and the *Annual Register* (1849). It fell upon a district of 400 square miles, and was 'the colour of ink, and of a fetid odour and very disagreeable taste'. Ireland was again deluged with a black rain on 30 April 1887 at Castlecomer, County Kilkenny. It was 'thick, black rain'. On 8 and 9 October 1907, another black rain fell in Ireland. This rain was reported to have 'left a most peculiar and disagreeable smell in the air'.

MICHAEL Costello (c. 1922–80), alias the Amazing Blondini, was born to entertain the public. His father was a strong man and his mother a fortune-teller. By the age of 13 he was a sword swallower. At 15 he could devour flaming torches. He could also chew up razor blades, electric light bulbs and thread needles through his flesh. Costello also specialised in blowing up coffins with explosives – while he was still inside.

~§

GLOVES manufactured in Limerick in the mid-19th century were so fine that a pair could be stuffed into a walnut shell.

~§

ON her death bed in February 1843, Miss Caroline Browne of Strabane, County Tyrone, aged 73, requested that she be buried with some locks of hair she owned in her left hand, and the remains of her pet canary in her right. A hoop ring of no great value was to be put on her ring finger and her favourite cap on her head. All her wishes were complied with.

~§

THE world's oldest known manuscript of the New Testament is in the Chester Beatty Library, Dublin.

~§

IN the Irish uprising of 1848, several leading rebels were captured, tried and convicted of treason against Queen Victoria. All were sentenced to death. Passionate protests from around the world persuaded the Queen to commute the death sentences. The men were banished to Australia. Years passed. In 1874 Queen Victoria learned that a Sir Charles Duffy who had been elected Prime Minister of Australia, was the same Charles Duffy, who had been banished from Ireland 26 years earlier. She asked what had become of the other eight convicts. She learned that Patrick O'Donahue had become a Brigadier General in the United States Army; Morris Lyene had become Attorney General for Australia; Michael Ireland succeeded Lyene as Attorney General; Thomas D'Arcy McGee became Minister of Agriculture in Canada; Terrence McManus became a Brigadier General in the United States Army; Thomas Meagher was elected Governor of Montana; John Mitchel became a prominent New York politician and his son, John Purroy Mitchel, a famous Mayor of New York City; and Richard O'Gorman became Governor of Newfoundland.

WHEN Aer Lingus recruited air hostesses in December 1945, a Russian princess was among the 900 applicants for the handful of jobs. Unfortunately, it was decided that only girls of Irish citizenship would be selected. The application guidelines stipulated that candidates should be aged between 21 and 25 years old, with a height of 5 ft 2 in to 5 ft 6 in, and weigh between 7½ and 9 stone. They were expected to be attractive and intelligent, and it was indicated that a knowledge of languages, especially French and Irish, while not essential, would be an important asset.

ISABELLA Laughin died on 25 April 1752 near Rathfryland, County Down, aged 118 years. Her grandfather and father were brogue-makers. She was married to a brogue-maker, her daughters were married to brogue-makers and her sons to brogue-makers' daughters. She was buried in a leather coffin, which was given by John Mercer, tanner of Newry, in appreciation of the family's loyalty to his business.

∼

IN November 1844 Ellen Rogers, aged 13, married Jeremiah Wilson in Crossmolina Church, County Mayo. She had previously rejected the attentions of four young men whose combined ages did not exceed that of the bridegroom.

∼

THOMAS Anthony McGroarty and his sister Annie Elizabeth of Ballinamore, County Derry are twins but were born in different years – Annie in 1939 and Thomas in 1940. Annie was registered as having been born at 11.30 p.m. on 31 December 1939, and Thomas at 12.30 a.m. on 1 January 1940.

∼

IN 1769 two widowers in County Tipperary entered into a unique pact. One was 69, the other 63. Both had numerous children who were all married except for one daughter each of about 18 years. In early June of that year they married each other's daughter. All lived together under the same roof. As an encouragement to procreation, the veterans made a bet of 100 guineas to be paid to the one whose young wife would first give birth and make the other a grandfather.

∽

TWO sisters, Anastasia and Mary Furlong of Bally-macroot, County Wexford, 103 and 105 years old respectively, died on 25 November 1841. They had lived and died together, and their mortal remains now occupy the same resting place.

∽

THE oldest footprints in the northern hemisphere are preserved in rocks near Valentia radio station in County Kerry, when a primitive four-legged, one-metre-long salamander-like creature walked along a mudflat while the tide was out. In 1992, the footprints were discovered by a Swiss geologist in rocks along the coastline. This internationally valued site is now protected by legisla-tion. Plaster casts of the fossils are on display in the geology museum in UCD and at the Heritage Centre, Knightstown, Valentia.

∽

A rare bird, bigger than a blackbird but of the same shape, with a white head and neck and a long white tail, made its appearance at Glendalligan, near Kilrossanty, County Waterford in early January 1946. Old inhabi-tants who saw the bird, which was thought to be from a northern region, said that it appeared only before a bliz-zard. It was known as the Blizzard Bird, and previously had been observed in the area before a big blizzard on 25 January 1916. It was recorded that one of these birds appeared before the big snowstorms of 1892, 1895 and 1900. Ireland experienced arctic-like conditions in the last few weeks of January 1946.

⸎

IN March 1766 Nicholas Sheehy (b. 1726) of Fethard, County Wexford was unjustly convicted and executed for murder. All 12 members of the trial jury subsequently died violent deaths.

⸎

FOR much of the 19th century, the world's finest collection of fossil fish was on display in Florence Court, County Fermanagh. The 10,000-strong collection was amassed by the 3rd Earl of Enniskillen, W. W. Cole (1807–86). The world's leading geologists visited the Fermanagh estate to study the earl's amazing collection in his private geological museum. The collection now belongs to the Natural History Museum in London.

⸎

IN August 1926, over the space of a week, Miss Anne Clarke of Raphoe, County Donegal single-handedly mowed, tied and stacked an acre of six-foot-high oats – at the age of 90!

⸎

THE first Duke of Wellington, the 'Iron Duke', became one of Britain's foremost statesman and military leaders. He could ride on horseback only by using a specially adapted saddle with a hole at the rear to accommodate a small, bony, vestigial tail which grew from the base of his spine.

⸎

ONE of Ireland's most remarkable heirlooms is a crystal ball handed down from generation to generation in the family of the Marquis of Waterford. It is reputed to cure cases of cattle disease. The ball of rock crystal, which is about the size of an apple, is in remarkably good condition despite being dropped and damaged in falls over the centuries. It is held together by a silver band. To effect a cure, the crystal is placed in a stream of running water and the sick cattle are driven through the water several times. The ball is believed to have been brought from the Holy Land at the time of the Crusades.

⤜

LOUGH Corrib in County Galway has known a number of great freeze-ups in its time. In the 1870s two men, roped together, skated from Galway to Cong – a distance of some 25 miles!

⤜

LORD Rokeby (1713–1800) was the only bearded nobleman of his time in Great Britain and Ireland.

⤜

UNTIL he died at the age of 104 in 1987, Ivan Beshoff was the last living participant in the famous mutiny of the battleship *Potemkin* in 1905, on which he was a stoker. He arrived in Dublin in 1913 with a letter from Lenin to the trade union leader Jim Larkin, who got him a job in the docks. During World War I Beshoff was arrested as a German spy and imprisoned in the Curragh. After the war ended Beshoff established a Soviet oil distribution company, but this enterprise later failed. In 1922 he set up his fish and chip shop on

Usher's Quay. Since then Beshoff's chippers have become a Dublin institution.

THOMAS Prendergast of Gort, County Galway, who fought in the War of the Spanish Succession, foretold in writing the date of his own death. On 11 September 1708, he recorded in his diary a dream in which a deceased servant had warned him of his death on that day 12 months later. One year later almost to the hour, Prendergast fell fighting the French at the Battle of Malplaquet.

A raised parapet road which crosses the sea between Brittany in north-western France and the island of St Cado was built by the Irish St Cado 1,400 years ago, yet is still in excellent condition.

NINE-year-old Irish boy Francis Seldon was imprisoned in the dreaded Bastille for making a pun about the king of France's bald head. The boy was a student in Clermont College in Paris. One day in 1674, King Louis XIV honoured the college with a visit. The school authorities were so overjoyed that they decided to rename Clermont and to call it 'The College of King Louis the Great'. Seldon was overheard telling a friend that since the king was bald, Clermont (the French for 'bare top') was already appropriate. Someone reported his pun to the school authorities. When the king heard it, he was furious. The king vindictively had a secret arrest warrant drawn up. Seldon remained in solitary confinement at the Bastille for 69 years. His wealthy family were told that the child had disappeared, so no one came looking for him. When Seldon was finally released he was a decrepit old man.

❧

ROBERT Russal (1744–71), a stonecutter of Newtownards, County Down, carved his own epitaph on a pillar in the local abbey when he was seemingly in perfect health and only 27 years of age – yet he died of natural causes and was buried beside the pillar only a few days later.

❧

AN assault trial was held in the Court of Assizes in County Donegal in 1835, in which the plaintiff, the defendant, the judge, the court clerk, both solicitors and all three witnesses were all named Doherty.

❧

THE world's largest free-hanging stalactite is located in the Pol an Ionain cave near Doolin, County Clare. The cave containing the 23-foot Great Stalactite is on land belonging to John and Helen Browne, who fought a 15-year battle to develop the cave as a tourist attraction, finally gaining planning permission in February 2005.

❧

AT the entrance to Castle Caldwell, near Lough Erne, there is a violin-shaped stone monument in memory of Dennis McCabe, a fiddler who fell out of a barge into the lake and drowned – and a warning to other fiddlers against over-imbibing whiskey. The weathered inscription from 1770 reads:

> *Beware ye fidlers of ye fidlers fate*
> *Nor tempt ye deep least ye repent too late*
> *Ye ever have been deemed to water foes*
> *Then shun ye lake till it with whiskey floes*
> *On firm land only exercise your skill*
> *There you may play and drink your fill*

~⑤

ARTHUR MacMurrogh Kavanagh (1831–89) of County Carlow, who was born with severely under-developed arms and legs, was one of the most remarkable men who ever lived. Through sheer determination and perseverance, he triumphed over his physical defects, learning to do everything an able-bodied person could do and to do it better. He taught himself to write 'in a good hand' by gripping a pen between his teeth. Strapped into a specially designed chair saddle, he quickly became an expert horseman, gripping the reins around his two arm stumps. Arthur trained himself to be a crackshot, using a gun without a trigger guard. He was able to hold the weapon under his left arm stump and squeeze the trigger with the other. He became a skilled yachtsman and a good angler fishing from a boat or even on horseback. He was a good amateur draughtsman and painter and a compulsive traveller. Famously, he undertook a three-year expedition with his brother travelling from Sweden to India on horseback and enduring many hardships. He returned to Ireland and became a much-respected progressive landlord and found time to serve in the British parliament for 14 years. Arthur married a beautiful young woman and became a father of seven healthy children.

᪥

DERRY-born pirate Darby Mullins (1661–1701) failed to heed his wife's warnings that he would die with his boots on. Just a moment before he was due to be hanged in London, he pulled them off, just to prove she was wrong.

᪥

A strange case of history repeating itself occurred on 24 October 2005, when an articulated lorry crashed into a railway bridge – for the second time in seven months. The same lorry had struck the same bridge at Park Road, Killarney on 15 March 2005, but a different driver was involved. The incident, which delayed road and rail traffic for several hours, occurred shortly before 2 p.m., around the same time of day as the previous one. The articulated trailer became stuck and quickly overturned, blocking the roadway and delaying overhead train services. The trailer was simply too high for the 4.65-metre bridge, gardaí said. No one was injured.

᪥

THE skeleton in the coat of arms of the city of Derry is a memorial to Walter de Burgh, whose skeleton was found in Northburgh Castle, County Donegal. He had been imprisoned there in 1328 and left to die of starvation by his own cousin.

᪥

IN *Anomalies and Curiosities of Medicine*, Gould and Pyle report the case of a teenage girl, Annie Jackson, who lived in Waterford during the 19th century and grew hideously misshapen horns from her 'joints, arms, axillae, nipples, ears and forehead'. Modern studies have revealed that the growth of horns is far more likely to occur in men than in women.

∽

THE first settler on the Galápagos Islands was an Irishman named Patrick Watkins. It is thought that he was marooned on Floreana Island in 1807. Watkins lived there for two years growing vegetables, which he exchanged with visiting whalers for rum. In 1809 he stole a whaling ship's long-boat and took five captured sailors with him as 'slaves'. When the boat reached the Ecuadorian port of Guayaquil, Watkins was the only one still alive.

∽

BOUTIQUE owner Maura Swan was late for work in Dublin on 9 June 2004 because her path was blocked by an angry namesake. Gardaí were called and took the swan back to the Tolka River. 'It was the most unusual arrest I've ever made,' said Sergeant Kiernan Kinsella.

∽

SAILOR Klaus Philippi mailed a postcard of the Eiffel Tower from Paris in September 1962 to his sister in Saarwellingen, Germany, using an Irish stamp by mistake, which probably explained the delay. Philippi's mother received it in August 2004 at the family home.

∽

IN the late 19th century, ether drinking was widespread throughout Ireland. One contemporary report estimated that one in eight of the population at the time were ether addicts. Ether vaporises at body temperature so drinkers had to develop a ritual to overcome this. They would rinse out their mouth with cold water, hold the nose and swallow the ether, quickly followed by more cold water. Regular etheromaniacs could sink a pint of the stuff a day in this way. If they failed to 'rift' (belch) at the appropriate moment, explosive vaporisation could cause a heart attack, and there were cases when people who rifted near naked flames had fire travel down their throats, causing them to explode.

A 12-inch-long brown trout, with a freshwater herring more than half its own length wedged in its gullet, was captured in the Lower Lake, Killarney in April 1929 by Mr P. O'Donoghue, who saw the fish in difficulties on the surface of the water.

THE first person to be awarded a Victoria Cross was Monaghan-born Charles David Lucas. On 21 June 1854, in one of the first engagements of the Crimean War, he threw an unexploded Russian shell from the deck of *HMS Hecla* during a bombardment in the Baltic Sea at the entrance to the Gulf of Bothnia. The shell actually exploded before hitting the sea, showing just how lucky Lucas had been. He was awarded the Victoria Cross on 26 June 1857 for his daring action, which saved the lives of many on board *HMS Hecla*.

❧

ON 1 September 1912, Captain Daniel Saunders of the *S.S. King Frederick VII* (outward bound from Belfast) fished a bottle from the sea containing a message dated 1 September 1872. The note asked the finder to notify the Belfast family of the Captain of the *Morning Star* that his wife had given birth to a baby boy that day. As fate would have it, Captain Saunders was that baby. He had the strange experience of being the first person to read of his birth exactly 40 years before.

❧

THE oldest harp still in existence in Ireland dates from at least 1300 and is kept in Trinity College, Dublin.

❧

ACCORDING to the Irish Seaweed Industry Organisation, over 560 types of seaweed grow in Irish waters.

❧

A stone wolfhound on the walls of Antrim Castle is a memorial to a wolfhound that saved Lady Marion Clotworthy from a wolf attack in the early 17th century and also alerted the castle to a sneak attack by an enemy force.

～

ON 29 May 1928, dozens of small reddish-coloured fish fell on the roof of a house in County Down during a thunderstorm. The owner, James McMaster, Drumhirk, near Comber, said they were mostly about two inches long. Surrounding hedges were blackened as if they had been struck by lightning. There was no river nearby, and Strangford Lough was over two miles away.

～

DANIEL McCarthy (1641–1752) from County Kerry married his fifth wife, a girl of 14, when he was 84. He lived another 27 years – and they had 20 children.

～

IN December 1835 the emigrant ship *Francis Spaight* was returning home to Limerick after a voyage to Saint John, New Brunswick, Canada when it was wrecked in the mid-Atlantic. There were 15 survivors left aboard the battered hull, but all the food and water had been washed overboard. Two weeks later the desperate survivors turned to cannibalism to survive. Lots were drawn among the ship's four cabin boys since the captain reasoned that they had no wives or children to support, unlike the other crewmen. The draw was apparently rigged, as 14-year-old Patrick O'Brien from Limerick (the most vocal opponent of what was happening) was selected to be killed and eaten first. Still protesting his fate, he was bled to death. Another unfortunate youth suffered the same fate before the remaining survivors managed to attract the attention of a passing American ship by waving O'Brien's hands and feet. No charges were ever brought against the boys' killers.

✎

NO one knows if frogs are a native species or were introduced to Ireland by the Normans. There is no mention of them in Ireland before the 12th century. Since the Normans were known to have introduced rabbits into the country, perhaps they also introduced frogs.

✎

DEATH had no terror for Bryan McMahon, an octogenarian from Sixmilebridge, County Clare. In October 1927 it was reported that he had just completed his earthly preparations for departure from this life, although he was still enjoying good health and carrying on his trade as a carpenter and builder. He had excavated his grave, erected a tombstone with a suitable inscription and had also constructed his own coffin. Mr McMahon was putting the finishing touches to his coffin when a correspondent of *The Irish Times* called on him at his workshop. When asked what had made him undertake this unusual task, Bryan set aside his paint-brush and replied: 'Well, I'll tell you. For years I have been troubled about it, and day and night I could not leave the thing out of my mind. Something was always prompting me that I should do the job. I was so worried and upset that finally I determined I would make a start, and, if God spared me life, I would finish it. I have it completed, and I feel as happy as can be now.'

⁓

IN 1946 aircraft ejector-seats were invented by Sir James Martin (1893–1981) from Crossgar, County Down. His invention was an instant success and quickly became a standard item in military jets worldwide. By the time Martin died, it is estimated that his invention had saved nearly 5,000 lives.

⁓

HAVING apparently spent four years in the Atlantic, a pint bottle sealed with a brass stopper was picked up in Tramore Strand, County Waterford in December 1928. Inside the bottle was a message written in pencil on a slip of paper. Although it was slightly faded, it was perfectly clear. On one side of it was written, 'Dropped about mid-Atlantic' and on the reverse 'Martin Heally, Nenagh, Tipperary, John Power, Fenor, Waterford, April 9, 1924.' Inquiries made with Harvey and Son, shipping agents, of Waterford showed that John Power, 20, of Fenor, Waterford, sailed from Cobh, County Cork for Halifax, Canada, on 6 April 1924, on the *S.S. Cedric*. The bottle contained only half a tablespoonful of water, and was picked up a few miles from John Power's home at Fenor.

⁓

IN early 1927, Dr Killen of the Belfast Eye, Ear and Throat Hospital successfully operated on an unnamed child's throat to remove a penny that had been lodged in its gullet for three months. If the object had not been removed, it would have eventually led to the child's death.

∽

IN June 1974 a block of ice, estimated to have weighed about 2 lbs, fell, burying itself into the lawns at the entrance gate of St Patrick's Hospital, Cashel, County Tipperary. The ice narrowly missed two of the maintenance staff who were working nearby. One of them, Thomas Furlong, said: 'It sounded like a shot.' A spokesperson for the meteorological office at Cashel imagined that the ice had fallen from a plane, but both witnesses said there was no plane around at the time. However, they did say that they had noticed a large black cloud overhead.

∽

WHILE shopping in a Dublin stationery store in 1870, Sergeant William Popple impulsively seized a saleswoman's cufflink and fled. After five years soldiering in India, he returned home to Dublin and tried to find the girl. Unable to recall the store, Popple visited every stationery store in Dublin until the cufflink was recognised by a saleswoman – whom Sergeant Popple promptly proposed to and married!

∽

PATRICK and Eleanor Grady, of Crookhaven, County Cork were born in the same house on the same day – 26 July 1700. They married on the same day, and 96 years later they both fell sick and died on the same day – leaving 96 descendants.

∽

WHILE strolling along a bank of the Borora River near Newcastle, Moynalty, County Meath in March 1936, Ronan Drury was attacked by an otter. The boy's hand was badly mauled and lacerated. He beat off the beast twice, but the otter returned, this time making for the child's neck. Help arrived from an unexpected source. A gander and a goose were swimming in the river and they viciously attacked the otter and beat it off, thus saving the child.

≪

SIR Hans Sloane (1660–1753) from County Down is responsible for the existence of the British Museum. He left his vast collection of books, manuscripts, gemstones, antiquities and plant and animal specimens from around the world to the British nation, provided it was kept together and held in London, where as many people as possible might see it. His conditions were accepted and money was raised to build a suitable venue to house the collection.

≪

THE world's least successful canal was built between Lough Corrib and Lough Mask in County Galway between 1848 and 1858. It is about three miles long and was considered a disastrous and costly failure. Genius engineers built it on porous limestone, which, as the name suggests, was less than watertight. When the canal was completed and water let in, it promptly drained away. In case you think this was purely an Irish folly, it should be remembered that the canal's designer was an Englishman, who altered the original plan, which would have seen the construction of a canal through an impervious layer of rock one mile to the west of the present canal. The only good thing about the canal was that it provided much-needed work in the locality during a time of great hardship.

❧

'HONEST Bill' Harwood, known as 'The Pilot of Dalkey', died in 1853, aged 101. He was a famous character who had once been blown in an open boat across the Irish Sea to Holyhead in Wales. All the celebrities of the day afterwards sailed in this boat, which was finally put to use as the roof of a summerhouse by a Dalkey tavern owner.

❧

NOT all actresses can cry to order and some directors have been known to resort to less than gentle measures to coax tears from the dry-eyed. Maureen O'Sullivan's tear ducts failed to respond in her deathbed scene as Dora Spenlow in *David Copperfield* (1935) until director George Cukor positioned himself out of camera range of the bed and twisted her feet sharply and painfully.

❧

GEORGE Bernard Shaw is the only person to have won both a Nobel Prize (for Literature in 1925) and an Academy Award (Best Screenplay for *Pygmalion* in 1938).

❧

HOW many people know of a place in Dublin where monkeys can be seen playing billiards? They are not live monkeys, nor are they stuffed. They can be seen every day outside the old Kildare Street Club premises, now part of the National Library of Ireland. On pillars near the windows at the bottom of Kildare Street are carvings of monkeys playing billiards, dating from 1860, by James and John O'Shea from County Cork. One is leaning over the table taking a shot, another one chalking his cue; still another is looking on with great interest. On a nearby pillar is a depiction of a greyhound racing, with an interested frilled lizard cheering on the winner.

~

IN August 1928, Antrim Magistrate W. J. Moore of Tir-Owen, Ashby Gardens, Belfast completed a circuit of County Down in a small homemade canvas canoe. Moore crossed Belfast Lough from Whitehouse to Bangor, and proceeded along the coast to Warrenpoint and Newry, returning to Belfast via the inland waterway to Portadown and the Lagan Canal, a distance of nearly 200 miles. He slept in his canoe at night.

~

BEAUTIFUL Belvedere House, near Mullingar, County Westmeath, was not always such a peaceful place. Robert Rochford, first Earl of Belvedere, accused his wife, Mary, of having an affair with his brother Arthur and imprisoned her in neighbouring Gaulstown House for over 30 years. She was guarded by mute servants who prevented her from escaping and stopped anyone visiting her.

~

ON 4 December 2001 the world record for the largest coin mural was set, consisting of an amazing 1,659,000 coins, and depicting a giant Irish coin. The Irish harp, since it appears on all coinage, is the main feature, and includes the dates 1995–2001. It was constructed at the National Museum, Collins Barracks, Dublin by members of Foróige, the National Youth Development Organisation, in aid of Pfizer Operation Rudolph, which supports many charities across Ireland. The former world record of one million coins was set in Minnesota in 1988 with a mural of Abraham Lincoln.

WHEN Irishman John McConnell turned up to fight Charley Davis for the English middleweight boxing title in London in 1873, he discovered that the bag containing his boxing gear had vanished. A lengthy delay ensued while substitute garments were produced until, to the vast amusement of the spectators, McConnell entered the ring wearing an old pair of cricket trousers which fit a man at least a foot shorter and about a foot wider. If this was not enough, McConnell also had no ice in his corner. During the contest, he floundered around the ring trying to hitch up his trousers, all the while sweating buckets. It was little wonder that the verdict went to his opponent.

FAMOUS Donegal-born actor Charles Macklin (c. 1690–1797) is said to have played the role of Shylock at the age of 99. His final performance was on 7 May 1789 in *The Merchant of Venice*. After stumbling through two or three speeches, he informed the audience that he was unable to continue.

LADY Luck shone on Cork woman Sinead Hudson when she found a five euro note on the roadside in late January 2004. She decided to spend it on a Lotto ticket. A short while later the 23-year-old was stunned to discover that she had won 200,000 euro!

※

WHEN the death of Colonel Blood, the County Meath would-be thief of the Crown Jewels, was announced, it was commonly believed that it was another trick of the notorious rogue. Just to be sure that he was really dead, the authorities exhumed the corpse a week later. When a jury of people who had known Blood examined the corpse, they had great difficulty agreeing that it was really him because his face had changed so much and was very swollen. They confirmed the corpse's identity after examining the thumb on its left hand, since Blood's was known to be twice the normal size.

※

THE cream cracker was invented in 1885 by W. R. Jacob at his premises on Bridge Street, Waterford.

※

WHEN Bryan Maguire's eldest son, George, died at the age of 12 in 1830, his father embalmed the body, using techniques he had learned in India. Maguire kept his son in a glass case, always by his side, up to the moment of his own death, five years later.

※

WIN or lose, after every fight Belfast flyweight Rinty Monaghan used to serenade the crowd over the ring microphone with a rendition of 'When Irish Eyes Are Smiling'. In fairness, he had more to sing about than most, retiring in 1950 as the undefeated world champion, having held the title for three years.

⤎

JOHN McNamara, of Scariff, County Clare, won the first frog-swallowing championship of Ireland at Ballycomber, County Offaly in 1975. He swallowed five live frogs in one minute, five seconds.

⤎

SIR Arthur Aston, the commander of the town of Drogheda in its resistance to Cromwell, was beaten to death with his own wooden leg when Cromwell's troops sacked the town in 1649. It was widely believed that Aston's wooden leg was hollow and filled with gold sovereigns, so when the soldiers captured him they wrenched off his leg. When they discovered that it was solid wood, there were so annoyed that they beat him to death with it. Aston's leather belt was found to contain 200 gold sovereigns, however, and the soldiers divided these among themselves.

⤎

THE oldest Irish mother recorded was Mrs Mary Higgins of Cork (b. 7 January 1876), who gave birth to a daughter, Patricia, on 17 March 1931 when aged 55 years and 69 days.

⤎

THE Irish rugby team of 1887 contained the Limerick forward John Macauley (1866–1958). He had been selected to play in the game against England, but was dismayed to discover that he had used up all his annual leave from work. A quick glance at his conditions of employment revealed that the only circumstances in which he could be granted additional leave was for a honeymoon, so he proposed to his girlfriend and fixed the wedding for the morning of the match. At the conclusion of the nuptials, Macauley and his new bride raced to Lansdowne Road in time for him to take his place in the Irish line-up.

❧

IN 1997, Lydia Foy grew a foxglove that reached a height of 3.29 m (10 ft 10 in) in her garden in Athy, County Kildare, setting a new world record. In July 2005 her record was beaten by 81-year-old pensioner Bill Leake from Agden, near Lymm, Cheshire in England, who grew a specimen that reached 3.6 m (12 ft). The normal height of foxgloves are 1.5 m (5 ft).

❧

AN Englishman, Derek King from Kent, was the first man to row around the entire Irish coastline. On 3 October 1971 he landed his craft, *Louise*, at Rossnowlagh, County Donegal having completed an estimated 1,500 miles in 108 days.

❧

THE world's largest collection of daffodils grows in a special garden at the University of Ulster, Coleraine.

Although daffodils are not native to Ireland, Irish plant breeders have led the world in developing new varieties. One of the most successful breeders of all time was Guy Wilson (1885–1962) of Broughshane, County Antrim. The Coleraine garden, created in Wilson's memory, was begun in 1971 in an old quarry and now has over 1,800 types of daffodil. Most were developed by Irish plant breeders, and the collection includes some unusual pink varieties bred by Waterford man Lionel Richardson.

❧

YEW trees are extremely long living – some are over 1,000 years old and they are the oldest living things in Europe. A yew tree at Muckross Abbey in County Kerry, reputedly planted in 1344, is said to be the oldest living entity in Ireland.

❧

THE first pig to fly travelled over England with Irish pilot J. T. C. Moore-Brabazon in 1909.

❧

ACROSS the street from Sligo Courthouse, a brass plaque still reminds passers-by that a remarkably named firm of solicitors, Argue and Phibbs, once practised there.

❧

IN 1896 caterpillar tracks, which enable machines to cross soft or rough ground, were invented by John Walker (c. 1841–1901) from Castlecomer, County Kilkenny. He submitted his invention to the War Office in London, but it had no interest in his invention. During World War I the military were forced to adopt caterpillar tracks because of the muddy conditions in the battlefields of Flanders. However, the War Office used a design patented by an English company in 1906, instead of Walker's system. His invention had more success in the United States, where his brother helped promote it.

~§

NEWGRANGE, an ancient burial mound near Drogheda, was built more than 3,200 years BC, predating both Stonehenge and the Great Pyramids of Giza.

~§

THE magnetic observatory at Trinity College, Dublin, now used as a weather bureau, was built in 1837 without the use of iron.

~§

CHRISTINE McDonnell from Dublin gave birth to a set of twins on 29 February 1956, and another set of twins on 29 February 1960.

~§

NOTORIOUS Fermanagh-born Bryan Maguire (c. 1780–1835) once fought a duel armed only with a billiard cue, while his opponent, one Captain Thurling, wielded a sword. Maguire escaped unscathed, but Thurling was fatally wounded. Maguire became addicted to duelling. His wife encouraged his hobby, to the extent of helping him with his pistol practice by holding – at arm's length – a lighted candle at which he would aim.

※

IRISH gambler Dennis O'Kelly (c. 1728–87) once owned a famous parrot which was able to whistle the 104th Psalm.

※

ON 3 May 1972, Patrick Donnelly of Belfast stopped to pick up a wallet he saw lying in the road. In order to find its owner, Donnelly leafed through the wallet, only to discover that the wallet belonged to another Patrick Donnelly, who lived in Augher, County Tyrone.

※

IN 1650, the Archbishop of Armagh, James Ussher (1581–1656), calculated that the earth was created on the evening before 23 October 4004 BC. To arrive at this conclusion, Ussher carefully counted the 'begats' in the Old Testament, studied numerous ancient Egyptian and Hebrew texts and analysed the various ways in which ancient calendars were calculated.

※

ON a summer's day in 1731, 21-year-old Kildare musician Jack Lattin danced his way along some eight miles of road between Morristown Lattin and Castle Browne in County Kildare, only to drop dead of exhaustion when he reached his destination.

※

DURING the 1641 Rebellion, Rory O'More of Balyna, County Kildare was one of the leaders of a plot to seize Dublin Castle. The conspirators were betrayed and only O'More managed to escape. His fellow conspirators were executed. He avoided capture by hiding in the thick woods around his family home. However, one day a force of English soldiers surprised him. He plunged his walking stick into the ground and fled from his pursuers. The stick took root and grew into a conifer. Family legend had it that when the tree died, the O'More family would leave Balyna. In 1957 the tree, a Scots pine, died and fell in a storm. The estate passed from the More O'Ferrall family shortly afterwards.

TO avoid the chaos of the 1798 Rising, Theobald Wolfe and his wife left their home in Blackhall, County Kildare and fled to Cheltenham. In their haste, Mrs Wolfe's pet terrier, Tip, was left behind. However, hardly had the Wolfes unpacked their bags in England than Tip came gambolling into their bedroom. He had followed them by road to Dublin, then caught a sailing boat to Holyhead and somehow tracked them down to Cheltenham.

ONE of the strangest guns ever invented was the .450 calibre six-shot revolver-folding dagger made by William Rigby & Co., Dublin (c. 1880–95). The ivory-handled pistol was a cruel-looking, seven-inch blade pivoted just behind the muzzle for ease of carrying. The curved blade was inspired by a Javanese weapon and had sharp saw-teeth at the rear to inflict serious damage. A lock kept the blade in place when extended or safely folded into a closed position.

DUNLUCE Castle on the County Antrim coast is one of the most picturesque ruins in Ireland. A tragic story tells how one evening in 1639, while hosting a large party, the hostess heard a rumbling sound and, upon investigating, the party found to their horror that a large portion of the kitchen, along with nine servants and much valuable plate, had fallen into the sea. A tinker, who was sitting on one of the windows mending a kettle, alone remained. The 'Tinker's Window' is there to this day.

❦

IN May 1929, newspapers reported the unusual sight of a hare chasing a greyhound at Dromoskin, County Louth. The leveret had been caught in a field six weeks previously, when it was only about two weeks old. Since that time it had been mothered by the dog. The two became inseparable. Every day the hare could be seen following its adoptive mother through the fields and along the roads. Although the greyhound, owned by Ted Murphy, had killed many rabbits and hares, she showed nothing but affection for the hare, which slept on the greyhound's back at night. When the leveret was caught, it was placed beside the greyhound, from whom pups had just been taken, and the dog adopted the hare as one of its own offspring.

❧

ON 26 February 1985 the *Daily Telegraph* featured a photograph of an aptly named Belfast shop. 'Reid & Wright' was a stationers and printers.

❧

MARY Young, alias Jenny Diver (c. 1700–41), from the north of Ireland, was a famous pickpocket and leader of a notorious gang of thieves. Not only was Jenny nimble-fingered, she was extremely inventive. She was an educated, attractive and well-dressed young woman who could easily mingle with the well-to-do without being suspected of being a thief. Jenny used this to her advantage on several occasions. The young Irishwoman is credited with inventing theft by 'false arms'. She frequented churches and theatres wearing a set of false arms, with her own arms concealed beneath her dress. Slits in the sides of the dress would enable her to 'relieve' those sitting around her of their valuables. Sadly, her long and profitable career came to an end on 18 March 1741 on Tyburn's scaffold. It is estimated that up to 200,000 people turned up to see the celebrity criminal be hanged.

❧

DURING the 17th century, church attendance was compulsory in Belfast. It was strictly enforced through penalties. For being absent from church, a householder was fined five shillings, a married woman half a crown, and every servant a shilling. No wine or ale was allowed to be sold during church hours.

✧

IN the 14th century, Bishop Richard Ledrede of Ossary tried to ban all secular songs and would allow only sacred music to be played.

✧

ONE of the strangest events in the history of Dalkey, County Dublin occurred in 1834, when a quarryman's daughter named Etty Scott dreamed that she saw a hoard of Danish gold buried under the 'Long Rock' on the seashore. This caused great excitement. Thirty-six men were persuaded to leave their work to dig for the treasure. Ballads were written and sung about this local Joan of Arc. Hundreds of people came from Dublin to see the excavations going on by torchlight, while on a rock above sat Etty Scott, a game-cock in one hand and a black-handled knife in the other, ready to shed the bird's blood when certain evil spirits were released from the rock. After a while, the workers found their efforts to discover gold unsuccessful. Some students finally exploded the myth in a cruel manner. They captured several cats, smeared their bodies with phosphorus and tied long strings, at the ends of which were sponges soaked in spirits of wine, to their tails. They then brought them in bags, by boat, to the seaward side of the 'Long Rock' and released them at night among the gold-seekers, having set the sponges alight. These horrible apparitions and the dreadful cries they emitted struck terror into the superstitious hearts of the workmen and they fled from the scene, but the bystanders quickly realised the joke. The ridicule brought to an end the dreams of Etty Scott, who died not long afterwards. Fortunately for the men who had abandoned their occupations to work for her, the value of land in Dalkey suddenly boomed, and because they had acquired portions of the shore for next to nothing, they were able to sell it at a good profit.

∽

IN the 1920s a certain bank in County Down had two unusually named employees. The cashier's surname was Speedy, and the cleaner was Mrs Slowly.

∽

AFTER spending the greater part of his life as a coastguard, Corkman Edward Jeffers took to travelling at the age of 84 and made a round trip of the world, leaving his home in Belfast on 1 January 1925 and returning in June 1926.

∽

IN 1935, Gerald More O'Ferrall of Lisard House in County Longford survived an assassination attempt by the IRA because a gold cigarette case in his dinner jacket had deflected the bullet.

∽

IN August 1927 Neal Boyce, of Aughavoy, Kilteevogue, County Donegal died at the ripe old age of 115. His daily food was potatoes, oat bread and oat porridge. He never knew what tea was until he was about 70 years of age. He could handle the scythe in the grass field when he was 105. The old man smoked a clay pipe, with strong tobacco, up to within a few days of his death.

~§

THE most famous castaway to have lived on Pohnpei in the Caroline Islands in the South Seas was James F. O'Connell from Dublin. After his ship was wrecked offshore in 1828, O'Connell and several other survivors reached land. It is said that the men's lives were miraculously spared by the islanders after the Irishman entertained them by dancing a jig. The lucky Irishman later married the pretty daughter of a chief and allowed himself to be heavily tattooed, according to island tradition. After O'Connell was 'rescued' in 1833, he went to America, joined P. T. Barnum's travelling carnival and became famous as 'The Tattooed Irishman'. He later wrote a fascinating book about his adventures, which is still an important source of information about the islanders.

~§

HARRY Badger was a famous eccentric in Cork City during the early 1800s. Dressed in yellow buckskin trousers, a red coat of vaguely military cut and a brass helmet bristling with iron spikes, he could generally be found lounging about near the old courthouse in South Main Street. His most celebrated characteristic was his placid indifference to what he ate or drank, and bets were often laid on how far he could be persuaded to go. A mouse was once slipped into his pint of porter. Harry saw it, but raised no objection and calmly finished his drink. His last meal was a bowl of strips of boiled leather in a milk and honey sauce. It took him two days to eat. On the third day he died.

❧

IN 1786 Roger Sweetman, a wealthy Irish merchant, built a replica of his Irish mansion, Blenheim Lodge in Ballymaclode, County Waterford, in Placentia, Newfoundland. All the building's materials were pre-cut or manufactured in Ireland and shipped over in Sweetman's ships. It is said that even the soil on the grounds around Blenheim House was shipped from Ireland.

❧

D. B. WALKINGTON (1867–1926), an Irish rugby player who represented his country between 1887 and 1891, was so short-sighted that he wore a monocle during matches. One writer says: 'He is as good as he can be on a bright day, but in the dark his sight tells terribly against him.' He is said to have removed it only when making a tackle!

❧

IN 1682, 12-year-old Dubliner Dick Bauf was found guilty of burglary and murder, alongside his parents, and was sentenced to death by hanging. In view of his youth, the boy was granted a full pardon on condition that he acted as his parents' executioner. At first Dick refused to carry out this barbaric act, but his parents, knowing that they were doomed in any case, persuaded him to see sense and live rather than share their dreadful fate. With his parents' blessing, Dick was their hangman, launching them into eternity. It is not surprising that Bauf grew up to become a notorious and merciless highwayman. At the tender age of 29 he was hanged on the same gallows in Dublin where he had executed his parents.

FAMOUS Waterford-born actress Dorothy Jordan (1762–1816) once received a plaintive note from her royal lover, the Duke of Clarence (later King William IV), asking her to accept a large reduction in the annual allowance he made her. Dorothy replied briefly by sending him a strip of paper torn off the bottom of a play-bill. It read: 'Absolutely no money returned after the rising of the curtain.' For over 20 years they were devoted to each other and their 10 children, until government pressure forced William to marry an unattractive German princess to provide a legitimate heir to the throne.

IN October 1737, the *Gentleman's Magazine* gave notice of an unusual marriage in Ireland between 'Andrew Newton aged 117, to a young woman of 19, who is big with child by him; he has a son living above 80, and is as hail and hearty as any man of 50 in the kingdom.'

IN 1240 the Abbot of the Cistercian Abbey of Knockboy, County Galway was severely censured for allowing a woman to wash his hair.

※

ON 12 February 1752, the Duke of Hamilton took one look at ravishing Irish beauty Elizabeth Gunning, and at midnight just 40 hours later he married the 17-year-old Roscommon girl in London's Mayfair Chapel. It happened with such speed that the groom didn't even have time to buy a wedding ring. Instead, he used a brass curtain hoop from his own bed. They were happily married until the Duke died seven years later. His widow quickly made it clear to all suitors that no one beneath the rank of duke need ask her out. In March of that year she married the handsome and very wealthy Duke of Argyll.

※

IT is said that the expression 'to chance your arm' is believed to have its origins in an event which occurred in St Patrick's Cathedral in Dublin. In 15th-century Ireland the two main political powers were the Butlers, Earls of Ormond, and the Fitzgeralds, Earls of Kildare. There were frequent disputes between the rivals but matters came to a head in 1492 when the Earl of Ormond's illegitimate nephew, Black Jack, arrived in Dublin with an army. Under the command of Gerald Fitzgerald, eighth Earl of Kildare, the Fitzgerald army routed the Ormond force. Fleeing from the enemy, Black Jack sought sanctuary in the Chapter House of St Patrick's Cathedral. Although he had the upper hand, Fitzgerald was shrewd enough to realise how politically beneficial it would be to end the feuding without further violence. Believing that he would be killed, Black Jack would not come out and negotiate a peace. Barricaded behind the Chapter House's thick oak door, he refused to budge. In order to end the standoff, Fitzgerald decided on a risky strategy. He had his soldiers cut a small hole in the centre of the door. Explaining that he wished for peace, the earl thrust his arm through the hole to shake hands with Black Jack. Rather than hack off Fitzgerald's arm (it must have been tempting), Black Jack shook his hand and ended the dispute. The Door of Reconciliation has been preserved and is now on display in St Patrick's Cathedral.

~&

AT one stage during World War II Ireland exported over 10 million rabbit carcasses a year to Britain.

~&

THE Reverend William Grey from Dublin introduced field hockey to Japan on 23 November 1906, when he founded the Keio University Hockey Club in Tokyo.

~&

ONE of the strangest documents existing from the Siege of Derry (1689) is a receipt signed by several notable defenders of the city, acknowledging the seizure of stocks of salmon belonging to Viscount Massereene.

~&

IN 1583 trial by combat was used to settle a court case between two chieftains of the O'Connor clan. Connor MacCormack O'Connor accused Teig MacGilpatrick

O'Connor of murdering men of his while they sought shelter with Teig. In his defence Teig claimed that the men had been communicating with rebels and were treated as such, and asserted his right for trial by combat – in other words, a fight to the death. Connor accepted the challenge and it was agreed that the matter would be resolved with swords in Dublin Castle the following day, in front of the Lords Justice and state council. The event took place according to the strict protocol and rules as laid down by law. After formalities, the two men took up their positions facing each other, stripped to the waist, armed only with a sword and shield. At the sound of a trumpet the fight began. Connor was wounded in the leg and eye. He tried to attack Teig, but his opponent was too strong for him and beat him back each time. A little later Teig won his acquittal, after decapitating Connor and presenting his head to the Lords Justice on the point of his sword.

A brief paragraph in the *Gentleman's Magazine* describes a rather hurried burial that took place on 15 July 1743: 'Died (in earnest) the wife of one Kirkeen, who was twice at Dublin to be buried; but came to life to her loving husband's great disappointment, who fearing the like accident immediately put her into a coffin, had it nailed up and buried her the next day.'

ACCORDING to a letter in *The Times* on 28 July 1990, a crop circle appeared on an uninhabited island in Roaringwater Bay, County Cork, where only rabbits would be able to see it. Officially Ireland's first crop circle appeared in August 1990, in a field of winter wheat in County Louth, belonging to Ardee farmer Billy Rogers. It was about 36 feet across and there was no sign of any access to it through the wheat.

❧

IN December 1907 the *Freeman's Journal* carried a report on the death of one 'Banker' Patterson, who left £80,000 to charity when he died. 'Banker' made his money by giving loans of single shillings, at one penny a week interest. He was illiterate and so miserly that he sat in the dark to save money, wore no trousers in summer, and his only possessions when he died were a cup, a plate and a knife.

❧

FOR many years until the late 18th century, public executions were carried out in St Stephen's Green in Dublin. In addition to hangings, there are records of criminals being burnt alive at the stake and being boiled alive.

❧

DURING his stay in Dublin in 1690, King William III presented a new mayoral chain to the Lord Mayor to replace the original one, which had been lost in 1688. The new chain is still in use.

❧

HENRY Temple, first Viscount Palmerstown (1673–1757), was appointed Chief Clerk of the Treasury of Ireland – at the age of seven. His father, John Temple, was speaker of the Irish House of Commons, and the appointment was a prime example of political patronage; it was worth nearly £2,000 per annum. Palmerstown held the position for the rest of his life.

✺

THE Lord of Tyrconnell, Turlough O'Donnell, who died in 1423, was the father of 18 sons by 10 different women. He had 59 grandsons.

✺

RACQUETS is a game similar to squash, but played with a hard ball. In the early years of the 19th century, one of the best players in Ireland was a Dublin tailor named Flood. He was extremely talented at racquets, but also lived a double life as a highwayman. Eventually he was caught and sentenced to death for his crimes. However, the then Lord Lieutenant of Ireland was a keen racquets fan and had heavily backed Flood to win a match against another highly rated player, Lord Sydney Osborne. With 1,000 guineas riding on the game, he pardoned Flood so that the contest could still take place. Full of gratitude to his unexpected saviour, Flood played magnificently and won. The Lord Lieutenant got his 1,000 guineas and Flood kept his life (and 50 guineas). Flood moved to London, changed his name to Waters and lived quietly as a marker at a racquets court in Tottenham Court Road.

✺

IN June 1928 it was reported that an epidemic disease had wiped out most of the cats in Strabane, County Tyrone.

Rats quickly overran the town. Cats from the countryside were brought in to boost the feline population.

❦

IN the 1830s, it was possible to travel from Ireland to England for nothing. A war between two shipping companies sailing from Liverpool to Belfast ended with one company carrying passengers to Ireland at three pence a head, while another company sailing to Waterford offered to carry people free. It is said that a rival company on the same route, not to be outdone, offered not only to carry passengers for nothing, but to give all passengers a loaf of bread. The other company then advertised that they would give to all who travelled in their steamers not only a loaf of bread, but a bottle of beer!

❦

DR PATRICK MERRIN of Dublin was famed 'for being the only survivor of a shipwreck from which nobody was saved'. Dr Merrin had agreed to act as medical officer to a 15,000-ton liner, *Waratah*, which was wrecked off the Cape of Good Hope in 1909 with no survivors. A week before its departure, personal circumstances compelled Dr Merrin to resign his position, and the ship sailed without him.

❦

IN March 1908 Mrs Mary Miskelly of Glastonkill, County Armagh lost her wedding ring while planting potatoes. In January 1950 workmen dismantling the chimney of a disused house on her farm pulled out the remains of a jackdaw's nest and discovered a glittering object amongst the twigs and hair. It was Mary Miskelly's lost ring!

❧

ACCORDING to those who have seen it, ball lightning is a terrifying sight. A luminous ball suddenly appears, advancing noisily towards the witness, occasionally burning people and objects, often disappearing after a violent explosion. On 22 September 1749 such a lightning strike devastated a house in Magherafelt, County Derry. In the middle of a terrible storm, ball lightning went down a chimney and into a room that was occupied by four people. A person sitting at the fire was lucky to escape with part of their clothes burnt. The lightning rolled about the floor for a moment, then divided in two. Another occupant suffered burns when one half exploded near them. The other part travelled through the floorboards to the room below, where there were two young women. What happened next was horrific: 'bursting with a great explosion, [it] struck one of them instantly dead; and tho' no wound appeared on the body, but part of her skin scorched as it were with gunpowder, yet the bones were all broken as if pounded.'

❧

KILKENNY man James O'Neill (1848–1920) was an extremely talented actor, but his claim to fame rested on one role. The handsome Irishman played the title role in the play *The Count of Monte Cristo* by Alexandre Dumas for over 30 years. During that time he criss-crossed North America and gave over 6,000 performances.

❧

LIEUTENANT Thomas Sweeny (1820–92) from County Cork joined the American army and distinguished himself during the US-Mexican War. At the Battle of Churubusco in 1847, he was badly wounded and had his right arm amputated. Despite this disability, he remained in the army, giving notable service throughout the American Civil War and retired in 1869 as a Brigadier General.

IN January 1960, 34-year-old Dundalk man Tony Watters averted a plane crash in Nova Scotia by hanging by his feet from the plane to secure a landing wheel. Watters, a sergeant in the Royal Canadian Air Force, was held by the feet by fellow crew members while he fixed the wheel in flight. The plane, carrying 20 people, had circled the landing field at Greenwood for three hours while the crew and ground officers were deciding what to do. Then the brave Irishman saved the day.

CORK eccentric Johnny Roche built himself a castle over a three-year period (1867–70). He completed this mammoth task solely with his own labour. He even invented a winch to haul up stones as the castle grew higher. The ruins of his castle still exist near Mallow. It consists of an oval tower 45 feet high and 27 feet long topped by two oval turrets that run at right angles to the main building. At the base of the tower a slab of granite is engraved with fine lettering: *John Roche, 1870*.

IN the 1920s it is said that the following notice was posted around an electrical station in County Donegal: 'Beware – To touch these wires is instant death – anyone found doing so will be prosecuted.'

❧

FARMER Robert Cook was the most startling figure of his time in Cappoquin, County Waterford. He never wore anything but white linen. Not only were his underclothes, night clothes and shirts in the purest white, but so were his suits, coats and hats. He became so famous for his clothes and passion for the colour white that he was known as 'Linen' Cook. He refused to have any black cattle on his farm and even his horses had to be white. Cook was a passionate vegetarian and refused to eat the flesh of any animal or wear anything produced by an animal. Instead of killing a captured fox which had attacked his poultry, he gave it a lecture on the evils of murder, then offered it a sporting chance by making it run through a line of his farm labourers, all armed with sticks. Cook was over 80 years old when he died in 1726. He was buried in a white linen shroud.

❧

IN 1996 a San Francisco bar and restaurant called the Bank of Ireland changed its name to the Irish Bank after the Bank of Ireland successfully sued it.

❧

THE oldest yacht club in the world is the Royal Cork Yacht Club, founded in 1720.

❧

THE Earl of Westmorland (1759–1841), Lord Lieutenant of Ireland from 1790 to 1795, was nicknamed '18 Pence' by the Irish because a shilling, worth 12 pence, was twice the size of a sixpenny piece, and the earl's right eye was exactly twice the size of his left.

※

ACCORDING to legend, the Red Hand became the symbol of the O'Neills when the founder of the clan was in a race with a rival Scottish chieftan to be the first to touch the Irish coast – the winner to have first claim on the territory. Since O'Neill was losing the race, he cut off his left hand and threw it ashore, thereby being the first to 'touch' the land.

※

FOR many years the Black Bell of St Patrick was displayed by the Gerarty family of Ballinrobe, County Galway. They charged visitors a fee to use it as a cure for rheumatism.

※

DURING the 17th century, Catholics and Nonconformists were not allowed into the walled town of Bandon, County Cork. The following notice is said to have been written on one of its gates: 'Jew, Turk or Atheist May enter here, But not a Papist.' Later this reply was posted: 'Whoever wrote this, Wrote it well, For the same is writ On the gates of hell.'

※

DUBLINER Alfred Rohu (c. 1860–1950) earned an international reputation as a naturalist, taxidermist and furrier. As a young man, he taught himself taxidermy, little knowing that this skill would come in handy. When he emigrated to South America to seek his fortune, his lack of Spanish handicapped his chances of employment in Buenos Aires. But when he presented a garden snail, perfectly stuffed to the very horns, to the curator of the museum in La Plata, Rohu's lingual deficiencies were overlooked, and he was employed on the spot. Eventually he returned to Ireland and set up his own business in his home city. Over the years, he stuffed everything that flew, swam or walked, from an angler fish to a 15-foot tiger, but he was still proudest of the snail.

◈

THE spectacular obelisk near Leixlip, County Kildare, known as 'Conolly's Folly', was erected for no purpose other than to give local employment during the famine of 1742.

IRISH immigrant Joseph Patrick O'Malley was electrocuted when he went walking beside the track of a New York subway railway line while drunk, and stopped to urinate. The stream of urine struck the electrified third rail and acted as a pathway for 600 volts to enter his body. The cause of his death became apparent only at the autopsy, when electrical burns were found on the tip of O'Malley's penis and on his thumb and forefinger.

A curious altar-tomb in Malahide Abbey, County Dublin contains the remains of Maud Plunkett, known as the heroine of Gerald Griffin's ballad of 'The Bridal of Malahide', and was said to have been a 'maid, wife and widow' in one day. Her husband died in a fray which took place immediately after the celebration of their marriage. Some say that she died of grief the same day, adding 'corpse' to the previous list. But other sources say that she lived to marry her third husband, Sir Richard Talbot of Malahide. The tomb is mounted by her effigy, depicted in the 15th-century costume of her day.

COUNTLESS numbers of people have seen the monument to the famous politician Charles Stewart Parnell at the junction of Parnell and O'Connell Streets in Dublin, but few will have noticed anything unusual about the statue. The statue, made by the famous Irish-born sculptor Augustus Saint-Gaudens, was erected in 1911. How many people will have spotted that it shows Parnell's curious habit of wearing two overcoats?

A bell taken from a wrecked ship of the 16th-century Spanish Armada still rings over the parish church of Donagh, County Donegal.

❧

IN June 1954, 8,000 racing pigeons vanished on their way from Milford Haven in Wales to Northern Ireland. Only 15 turned up, exhausted, at their destination. Six more in the same condition were found in Swansea, to the east of Milford Haven.

❧

MONKSTOWN Castle, County Cork was built in 1636 by Anastatia Archdekan, at a cost of fourpence. She made her workmen buy all their food and clothing from her stores, thereby recovering all but fourpence on her outlay.

❧

IN September 1928, Englishman Carl Williams was fishing for pike on Lough Derg when he caught a one-pound perch and a cormorant which had swallowed the perch just after Williams had hooked it. The cormorant itself was hooked by its catch.

❧

ROBERT Rochford fell out with his brother George, who lived nearby within sight of his home, Belvedere House in County Westmeath. Robert hated to have his brother's house in constant view, so, around 1760, he decided to build a sham ruin to block out the sight. At great expense, he imported a number of Italian artists to Westmeath to build a remarkable ruined abbey complete with Gothic windows to stand between him and his brother. It is known as the Jealous Wall.

᠅

ON 18 October 1984, five circus lions escaped from Chipperfield's Circus in County Wexford, causing a short-lived panic. Three were quickly caught. The other two were rounded up after four hours. One had been hit by a car and the other was cornered in a farmyard.

᠅

IRISH rugby international Basil Maclear, who was capped 11 times between 1905 and 1907, liked to cut a dash on the field and frequently played in expensive white calfskin gloves. Once, in a game against Wales, he made a further fashion statement by donning military puttees.

᠅

ON 27 April 1974 a car knocked down six-year-old Norbert Burke as he was playing near his home in Limerick, marking the start of a bizarre triple tragedy. The 44-year-old father of the boy was brought to the scene and collapsed. He was rushed to a nearby hospital, where he died of a suspected heart attack. The driver of the car, farmer George Leonard, 45, also collapsed when he saw the dead boy. He was rushed to the same hospital, where he too died.

᠅

IN November 1987, a wildlife ranger discovered a six-month-old American bald eagle in County Kerry.

Eddie the Eagle, as he came to be known, was starving and exhausted. He quickly became front-page news, earning a reputation as the first American eagle to make it across the Atlantic to Europe. He returned to the United States in style, travelling first class on a transatlantic jet. Even Charles Haughey, the then Taoiseach, showed up at Shannon Airport to see Eddie off. After a safe flight, Eddie, now renamed Iolar, settled into a wildlife reserve in Massachusetts, unaware of the controversy he had left behind. Doubts that such a young bird could have flown 3,000 miles across open ocean emerged, especially in the light of evidence that clearly showed that bald eagles can fly no more than 200 miles at a stretch. Members of the Irish Hawking Club speculated that the bird had been illegally imported from West Germany and released into the wild after its owner had failed to find a buyer. A spokesperson for the Irish Hawking Club confirmed that members had heard that an eagle had been offered for sale in Ireland, thereby providing the most likely explanation for his appearance in the country.

A tailor called Patrick Redmond was hanged on Cork City's Gallows Green on 10 September 1766 for robbery. After 28 minutes, the mob rescued the body and carried it to an appointed place, where a surgeon performed a bronchotomy, an incision in the windpipe. In less than six hours, Redmond was brought back to life. A collection was made for him, along with moves to obtain a pardon, for English law said that the condemned shall hang until he is dead. Those, like Redmond, who recovered were liable to be strung up again.

⌘

IN the *Gentleman's Magazine* of July 1731, it was reported that Jane Hook of Belfast, aged 112, 'had lately all her old stumps drove out by a new set of teeth; which were more welcome, because the account affirms her appetite and other faculties are as good as when she was but 20.'

⌘

DUBLINER Sir Charles Cameron, in his 1921 autobiography, recorded that his white hair returned to its normal colour after an accident had confined him to bed for some months in his 80th year. He also refers to a man of 90 having his hair return to its natural brown.

⌘

PEOPLE were just as cynical about morality in the 18th century as they are today. Jonathan Swift wrote that 'an old gentlewoman died here [in Dublin] two months ago, and left in her will to have eight men and eight maids as coffin bearers, who should have two guineas (£2 2s.) a-piece, 10 guineas to the parson for a sermon, and two guineas to the clerk. But bearers, parson and clerk must all be true virgins, and not be admitted till they took their oaths of virginity; so the poor woman lies still unburied, and must do so till Resurrection Day!'

⌘

IN an 1805 issue of *Wonderful and Scientific Museum Magazine*, 70-year-old Elizabeth Westly from Macroom,

County Cork earned a special mention. From about 1798 onwards, she had suffered from a considerable degree of pain on one side of her head, from which a horn, resembling in shape and substance that of a ram, grew to a length of nine inches. After feeling a similar sensation on the opposite side of her forehead, she believed that a horn had started to grow on that side too.

✧

DURING an operation on a nine-year-old Derry boy suffering from appendicitis, the operating surgeon was surprised to discover that the boy had a full-grown hazelnut, complete with shell, lodged in his appendix! The operation to remove the appendix, performed in Derry Infirmary in March 1927, was a complete success. The appendix – with the nut inside – was preserved for the boy to keep as a memento.

✧

IN October 1673, during a great storm, a strange giant squid was driven ashore at Dingle, County Kerry. Nineteen feet long, its broad body was fringed with an undulating fin, similar to that of a cuttlefish. 'It swoom by the lappits of the mantle', according to showman James Steward, who exhibited parts of the creature. He claimed that it had two heads, one large and one small: 'the little head could dart forth a yard from the great, and draw it in again at pleasure.' The eminent Victorian zoologist A.G. More, recognising the 'little head' as something else entirely, was apparently much impressed by this feature of the Kerry monster because he named it *Dinoteuthis proboscideus*.

✧

FROM 1982 to 1984 villagers in a part of west Donegal were terrorised by a spate of freak lightning bolts. Roofs were stripped off houses in 10 villages. Windows were also smashed, pipelines wrecked, telephones and television sets blown up. On Christmas Day 1984, lightning turned the area's first white Christmas in 20 years into a three-day blackout. No one knows why storms have chosen to blast this particular area. All that the villagers could do was to petition the government to fit lightning conductors onto the roofs of their houses.

❧

IN March 1985, 24-year-old Paul James from Shangarry, County Carlow defied death after drowning in an Amsterdam pond. He was declared clinically dead for 12½ minutes, but was brought back to life by a heart specialist just seconds before brain death. James had fallen into the freezing water while trying to save his dog. He was 23 minutes in 5 feet of water before being rescued. It later emerged that his rescue had been hampered because his dog would not allow fire brigade personnel near him. The dog had had to be knocked out with a tranquilliser before they rescued James. The young Irish emigrant was in hospital for two days before he could be identified. Eventually the hospital established his identity through information on his pet's collar (the dog also survived), and police broke into James's flat and found his identity papers. He suffered no permanent damage but spent two months in hospital recovering from his ordeal after contracting several viral infections.

❧

HENRY Eeles (c. 1699–1781) from Lismore, County Waterford invented a sailing boat that was equally at home on dry land as it was at sea. His ingenious amphibious contraption was an ordinary boat fitted with sails, but it had one major difference – it was fitted with large wheels! Eeles used to sail his 'sailing coach' on the open expanses around Lismore and became quite adept as a dry land sailor using the boat's hind wheels to steer. He often gave demonstrations to the curious. One day he had the 'sailing coach' on Youghal Strand, with several passengers, when, as they were moving along quite comfortably, he suddenly put the helm hard down and dashed the coach into the sea, to the great alarm of his guests. The coach was, however, quite watertight and sailed with as much ease and safety as she did on dry land. Eeles took out a patent for this extremely useful invention, but it never caught on.

DUBLIN Bay prawns do not come from Dublin Bay and they are not prawns. True prawns have a soft transparent shell, but the Dublin Bay prawn has claws and a hard pink shell that it sheds regularly as it grows. In other words, it is more like a small lobster. It is found in the Irish Sea north of Lambay Island, along the west coast of Ireland, around Scotland and in the Atlantic Ocean from Iceland to Morocco and even into the Mediterranean – in fact, almost everywhere except Dublin Bay, where sediment makes it an unsuitable habitat. It is also called Norwegian lobster or langoustine. Thankfully, you can avoid confusion by using its scientific name, *Nephrops norvegicus*.

SIR HANS SLOANE (1660–1753) from Killyleagh, County Down invented drinking chocolate when he was in the Caribbean. Sloane was introduced to the local cocoa drink during his stay in the islands, but added milk to make it more palatable and brought the drink to Europe. In London, apothecaries sold his drinking chocolate as a remedy, and Cadbury's popularised it.

⁓

IN January 1793, *Wonderful and Scientific Museum Magazine* reprinted an article from an earlier issue: 'Remarkable relation of a dog swallowed by an eel. A gentleman in the province of Leinster in Ireland in December 1749 fired at a duck on a lake that was frozen over; the duck being only wounded, dived under the ice, the gentleman's dog following her, but not returning, he went home. In the month of February following, a fisherman having caught a prodigious large eel, many people went to see it, and among the rest the above gentleman. The fisherman agreed to open the eel, when to the surprise of all the spectators out jumped poor Tray, the gentleman's dog, and ran fawning to his master brisk and lively, but greatly emaciated, from remaining so long in the eel's belly.' It is easy to dismiss this tale, but it may be a distorted version of an actual event. In October 1987 a similar story emerged from northern Siberia. A fisherman's dog disappeared while swimming in the same river in which the man was fishing. Moments later the fisherman cast his net and hauled in a large pike, 5 ft 8 in long, weighing 114.6 pounds, with a tail sticking out of its jaws. The fisherman cut it open and his dog struggled out, barking and apparently none the worse for its experience.

❧

A remarkable example of a master's affection for his dog occurred when Colonel Cecil Browne-Lecky of County Derry died in January 1927. In the summer of 1925, when the Colonel was on holiday at Greencastle, County Donegal, he learned of the death of his favourite water spaniel, 'Peter'. He cut short his holiday and immediately returned home, to find the servants making arrangements for the disposal of the dog's body. The Colonel ordered a specially lined and padded coffin, and into this Peter's remains were placed. The coffin was borne on the shoulders of employees to the estate's churchyard, where it was buried in the family vault. The Colonel had the following inscription placed on a brass plate on the dog's coffin: 'In memory of Peter, a faithful dog and friend to Colonel Browne-Lecky D.L.J.P. "Such was my dog, who now without my aid hunts through the shadowland, himself as shade; or, crouched perchance before some ghostly gate, awaits my step as here he used to wait."'

Only one more space remained in the vault after Peter's interment. Browne-Lecky reserved it for himself, taking care that Peter's coffin was deposited so that when the Colonel was called to rest, Peter would be reclining at his feet. Eighteen months later the Colonel died; he was laid to rest in the family vault beside his ancestors and Peter.

❧

IN January 1927, a Tyrone man and woman, whose ages totalled 201 years, figured in a pensions claim at the meeting of the Strabane and Donemona old-age pensions committee. When Mrs Mary Jane Thompson (99) of Drain, Donemona applied for a pension, her claim was supported by John Blee (102), also of Donemona. Having given his age, Mr Blee confirmed that he had known Mrs Thompson since childhood. The committee granted the pension.

IN September 1989, Vincent Balfe, a farmer from Rathvilly, County Carlow, spent three weeks searching for a missing two-year-old pure-bred Charolais heifer called Dreamer. Eventually he decided he must have sold her by mistake at a local cattle market. Five months later, as the farmer's hayshed was being cleared, Dreamer emerged from among the bales. It was thought that the animal had wandered into the shed while the straw was being stacked. The heifer had lost 450 pounds during its captivity, but she had eaten some straw, twine and all, and had apparently managed without any liquids. Tommy Murphy, a local vet, said: 'It was as if it had hibernated. It could stand, and while thin, was not emaciated.' She soon put on 100 pounds and appeared to be none the worse for her experience. How did Dreamer survive so long without water? It was thought that she got enough water from her surroundings when it rained and water pooled on the ground.

A butcher from Waterford City called Henry Denny invented bacon rashers in 1820.

IN 1986 a notice in the maternity unit of the Belfast City hospital warned the staff: 'The first five minutes of life are the most dangerous.' Underneath someone subsequently wrote: 'And the last five are pretty dicey too.'

⤚⟡⤙

FEW realise that a handful of Irishmen have lived Robinson Crusoe-like lives on islands in far-off corners of the world. In 1823, 28-year-old County Down convict Alexander Miller escaped the penal colony of Van Diemen's Land (Tasmania) by stowing aboard the sealing ship *Caroline*. After collecting a full cargo of elephant seal oil, *Caroline* returned to Sydney, leaving Miller behind on Macquarie Island. Miller spent two cold, hungry and lonely years battling for survival on the island, before deciding that this dreadful 'freedom' was not worth its price. When another sealing ship arrived, he asked them to take him back to Hobart with them. On his return to Tasmania, Miller received 50 lashes and was sent to a nearby island penal settlement. Miller did not give up his attempts to escape from Tasmania. He next tried to stow away on a ship which was heading to warmer climes than Macquarie Island, but he was captured before the ship left the Hobart docks. He was sentenced to three months in a chain gang and 14 days on the tread wheel. Over the following years Miller had many charges of drunkenness recorded against him before he received a conditional pardon in January 1845 and slipped into obscurity.

⤚⟡⤙

IN early 1796 an extremely wealthy but gullible Dublin umbrella-maker was persuaded to pay well over the odds for a three-acre plot in Blackrock, because the seller assured him that the land was particularly well suited for growing whale-bone from cuttings. The unsuspecting businessman had half an acre planted with pieces of whale-bone in the hope of a plentiful crop, before a friend brought the foolish man to his senses.

~§

UP until a few days before her death in February 1928, 105-year-old Bridget McKenna of Tavneymore, County Tyrone was able to thread a needle without spectacles. Her father had lived to be more than 100 and her younger 98-year-old sister survived her. Bridget McKenna had enjoyed remarkable health throughout her life and was 'possessed of all her mental faculties in the fullest degree'. She had never been in a car or on a train.

~§

IN 1537 William Grant, a soldier trapped atop a flaming tower of Dunashad Castle, Baltimore, County Cork was saved by an enemy bowman named John Butler. Butler attached a length of rope to one of his arrows. Grant tied the rope to the battlement and slid to safety inside the castle walls.

~§

OWEN FARRELL (c. 1716–40) from County Cavan was a famous dwarf. Despite his small stature – he was only 3 ft 9 in – Farrell was capable of incredible feats of strength. One account says that he 'became celebrated by allowing a cart to be driven over his chest and a Blacksmith's anvil to be placed upon his breast while in a horizontal position, resting his head and heels upon two chairs, and the anvil to be then hammered on with the Great Hammer in the usual way.' Another account says that Farrell was so strong 'he could carry four men, two sitting astride on each arm.'

⁓

FOR a brief period, the world's least convenient post box was located at Ballymacra, County Antrim. In March 1979 workmen replaced a telegraph pole upon which the local pillarbox was fixed. The workmen did not have the keys needed to release the clips that fastened the box to the pole, so they raised it over the top of the old one and then slipped it down the new one. The new pole turned out to be thicker than the old one and the post box came to rest nine feet above the ground. It remained in this position for three weeks, during which time post still managed to get through – someone had kindly provided a stepladder!

⁓

THE first magpies in Ireland arrived in County Wexford. They were reputedly blown across the Irish Sea during a storm in the early 1680s. Colonel Solomon Richards of Wexford town recalled in 1682 how: 'There came with a black easterly wind, a flight of magpies, under a dozen as I remember, out of England or Wales, none having been seen in Ireland before. They [a]lighted in the Barony of Forth, where they have bred and are so increased that they are in every wood and village in the County. The natural Irish much detest them, saying "they shall never be rid of the English while these magpies remain".'

≤§

IN the middle of the 19th century a well-known character named Supple Jack lived in Castlegregory, County Kerry. He never wore shoes or stockings and was usually clothed in an old red coat and shorts, with a fox-skin cap on his head, emblematic of his calling – he made his living by trapping foxes. Supple Jack carried a bundle of blackthorn switches. He bound these together by splicing them like a fishing rod, and used them to draw the young cubs out of the 'earth' by entangling the switches, which were well covered with thorns, in their fur. To do this, he had to crawl some way into the fox's den, so it was just as well that he was a small and presumably 'supple' man. His occupation was not without risk. On one occasion the tunnel collapsed behind poor Jack, entombing him for three days. He was a man of strong nerves; when he was rescued, his first thought was to secure the vixen and four cubs which had nearly cost him his life. At times he would have as many as 15 brace of foxes in his kennels and had no shortage of buyers.

≤§

ON 9 June 1860 a large sandstone pebble, 'about the size of a duck egg', fell from the sky at Raphoe, County Donegal.

≤§

IN late March and early April 1911 there were several reports of a strange immigration of vast flocks of birds in the south-east and east of Ireland. The most feasible explanation given for this phenomenon is that the birds were migrants, which had been driven from the Continent by a sudden fall in temperature. One of the strangest reports of these vast flocks was given by the captain of a steamer on the Irish Sea. Captain Kirwan of the *Colleen Bawn* described a bizarre episode that would not have been out of place in Alfred Hitchcock's eerie film *The Birds*. Kirwan's ship was accompanied by innumerable birds from Drogheda to Liverpool on the 29 March sailing and also on his return trip the following day. This enormous flock hovered round the steamer every inch of the way. Those that could find a spot perched on every available part of it, including the funnel, while the rest flew around the ship.

✧

ON 12 and 14 October 1621, the airspace over Cork City was the battleground for a civil war amongst thousands of starlings. For days before the battle commenced the city's inhabitants watched two enormous flocks of starlings assemble, one to the west and the other to the east of the city. The birds behaved unusually and made strange calls and cries that people had never heard before. It seemed to onlookers that parties of negotiators, about 20 or 30 in each group, regularly flew between each army. These avian diplomats would hover over the opposing force and emit strange calls and cries before returning to their own side. At nine o'clock on the sunny morning of 12 October, the battle commenced:

'Upon a strange sound and noise made as well on the one side as on the other, they forthwith at one instant took wing, and so mounting up into the skies encountered one another, with such a terrible shock.' Many dead or badly wounded starlings fell from the sky over Cork. The battle raged all day and well into the night, then something unexpected happened: the starlings disappeared. Next day there was none to be seen in or around the city. Where had all the birds got to? Nicholas Bourne wrote a pamphlet called *The Wonderful Battel of Starelings, Fought at the Citie of Corke, in Ireland, the 12 and 14 of October, 1621*. Bourne investigated the strange events and collected evidence and statements from many eyewitnesses. Bourne believed he had solved the mystery when correspondents reported the occurrence of a battle of thousands of starlings over the Thames estuary, east London, on the day following the Cork battle. The starlings returned to their previous battleground over Cork the next day and the wide-ranging civil war continued unabated. More dead and wounded starlings rained down on the city and locality. Strangely, a kite, a raven and a crow lay amongst the casualties. For centuries

unusual occurrences in the natural world (such as bird battles) were believed to be an ominous sign of ill tidings to follow. This certainly was the case in Cork. Almost a year after the strange battle, Bourne issued another pamphlet, concerning what he believed the battle portended. It was an account of 'the most Lamentable Burning of the Citie of Cork by Thunder and Lightning, with other most Doleful and Miserable accidents, which fell out the Last of May 1622 after the Prodigious Battell of the Birds called Stares'.

⤛

A Lisburn steeplejack had a miraculous escape from death in late December 1910. He was working on a 260-foot chimney belonging to Barbour's thread works when he lost his grip of a rope just 10 feet from the top and tumbled to almost certain death. The steeplejack was just 14 feet from the ground when he struck a steam pipe, which pitched him into a nearby tree. He landed lightly on a grassy lawn without even receiving so much as a scratch and went back to work shortly afterwards.

⤛

ACCORDING to the 1999 *Oxford Dictionary of Idioms*, the expression 'son of a gun' most likely gets its origins from babies born at sea to women who were allowed to accompany their husbands on naval ships. A little-known fact is that the saying actually originates in the heart of Dublin. In 1705 a very interesting book called *The Life and Errors of John Dunton* was published. This is the passage in which the first ever use of the expression occurs: 'The first visit I made in Dublin (about 1699) was to Nat Gun, a bookseller in Essex Street, to whom I was directed by my friend, Mr Richard Wilde, whom I had left behind me in London. This son of a Gun gave me a hearty welcome, and, to do him justice, he is as honest a man as the world affords: and is so esteemed by all that know him.'

ACCORDING to legend, the splendid bells of St Mary's Cathedral in Limerick have a romantic but tragic origin. It is said that long ago they were made by an Italian craftsman for an Italian convent. For many years, the story goes, this man toiled at the bells, in which he took great pride, and they were eventually installed in a neighbouring convent. With the profits of the sale, the Italian bought a villa where he could live in peace and listen to the peals of his beloved bells. His peace was short-lived, however. He lost everything, the convent was razed to the ground and the bells carried to another country – Ireland. The craftsman, haunted by the peals of the bells, wandered throughout Europe, and so grew to be old and withered. Having scraped together some money during this time, and feeling himself sinking slowly in health, the old man resolved to hear his bells once more before he died, and, with this objective in mind, started out for Ireland. He sailed up the Shannon and anchored near Limerick, where he hired a small boat to land. The old town lay before him, and he could see the steeple of St Mary's rising above the smoke of the historic city. Contemplating the scene, he was reminded of his old Italian home. The Shannon was like a sheet of glass; his boat drifted easily along in the summer evening, and everything was silent and still. Suddenly the calm was broken by the crash of the cathedral bells. The old man stirred, as if settling himself more comfortably, and so listened to his long-lost bells. They found him later with his face turned towards the cathedral, but his eyes were shut. He was dead.

᪐

ON 27 July 1875 small masses of damp hay fell out of the sky at Monkstown, County Dublin.

᪐

THE skeleton of the Irish giant Cornelius McGrath (7 ft 2.25 in), who was born in Silvermines, County Tipperary in 1736 and who died in 1760, is kept in the Anatomy Museum in Trinity College, Dublin.

᪐

IN the 1879 volume of the London *Hospital Gazette*, Dr Jewett recorded the case of an Irish drayman who went without treatment for 47 days after receiving an extreme wound to his skull. The penetrating wound was a quarter inch in diameter and four inches deep. The man made a complete recovery, in spite of the delay in receiving treatment.

᪐

THE largest recorded meteorite to fall in Ireland was a stone of 65 lb (29.5 kg), part of a shower weighing more than 106 lb (48 kg) which fell near Adare, County Limerick on 10 September 1813.

᪐

IRELAND'S rarest fish is possibly the Goureen or Killarney Shad (*Alosa Fallax Killarnensis*), which is found in Lough Leanne, Killarney and nowhere else in the world.

~§

LAOIS is the only county in Ireland that is surrounded by inland counties – Offaly, Kildare, Carlow, Kilkenny and Tipperary.

~§

IN the summer of 1748 a shower of a yellowish substance, resembling brimstone, fell on the town of Doneraile in County Cork. It had a sulphurous smell and thinly coated the town and surrounding area for a brief period before quickly dissolving.

~§

IN the 1879 Philadelphia *Medical Bulletin*, Dr Colton wrote about a 23-year-old Irish girl who had an incredible painless labour: 'She felt a desire to urinate, and while seated on the chamber dropped a child. She never felt a labour-pain, and 12 days afterward rode 20 miles over a rough road to go to her baby's funeral.'

~§

RICHARD Bourke, the 6th Earl of Mayo, was assassinated in 1872 when he was serving as Viceroy of India. His body was transported home in a large cask of rum for interment in Johnstown, County Kildare, earning him the nickname 'The Pickled Earl'.

~§

IN the 1857 edition of the *New York Journal of Medicine*, a Dr Corson wrote about the strange case of an Irishman who suffered from exhausting hiccoughing for four months. The cause was extreme fright.

⤚⤙

THE Female Oddity lived on the outskirts of Dublin, and wore only green-coloured clothes. According to the *Gentleman's Magazine* for 1780, she was not too particular about what she ate. 'A fricassee of frogs and mice is her delight. Loves beef and mutton that is flyblown; when a child she used to be found eating small coal, and at night if her mother left her in her room by herself, she was seen to dispatch all the contents of the candle snuffers.'

⤚⤙

AS a result of a childhood injury, Hugh Montgomery, Earl of Mount-Alexander (1626–63) from County Down, had a large opening on the left side of his chest. This cavity provided a large enough 'window' to clearly view his beating heart. Montgomery wore a metal plate over the opening to protect his heart and lived a full and active life. He became commander-in-chief of the Royalist army in Ireland and led cavalry charges during the campaigns against Cromwell. King Charles II introduced Dr William Harvey (1578–1657) to Montgomery. This meeting gave the famous doctor a unique opportunity to actually see a living heart beating in a healthy body. Harvey later wrote that he inserted 'three forefingers, and my thumb' and 'took notice of the motion of his heart'.

⤚⤙

THE slow-worm is common all over Britain and the entire European continent, but it is found in Ireland only at a few sites in the Burren in County Clare. It is not clear if it is a recent introduction or a native Irish species. The first definitive recording of its presence in Ireland was in 1977. Although the slow-worm is a lizard, it might easily be mistaken for a snake because it has no legs. It is harmless to humans and lives on slow-moving prey such as slugs and earthworms. It hibernates in winter and is long-lived.

IN 1658 Waterford evangelist John Perrot visited Rome with the hare-brained intention of converting Pope Alexander VII to the Quaker faith. For his efforts, he was thrown in jail. He languished there for three years at the hands of the infamous Inquisition.

RICHARD POKRICH (1690–1751) from County Monaghan invented musical glasses and earned himself worldwide fame. His invention, 'The Angelic Organ' as he called it, was a series of large glasses individually filled with varying quantities of water which produced sublime music. On at least one occasion his invention helped the eccentric inventor escape prison. According to Peter Somerville-Large's wonderful book *Irish Eccentrics*, the musical glasses' 'sweetness lulled two bailiffs' who had come to seize him for bad debts. 'Gentlemen,' Pokrich told them, 'I am your prisoner, but before I do myself the honour to attend you, give me leave, a humble performer in musick, to entertain you with a tune.' 'Sir,' one of the bailiffs answered, 'we came here to execute our warrant, not to hear tunes.' But with the bribe of a bottle of fine wine, Pokrich persuaded them to sit and listen to his favourite tune, 'Black Joke'. He gave such a wonderful performance that the bailiffs let him go, on the understanding that he keep their actions a secret.

❧

DURING the Crimean War, Corporal John Lyons from Carlow won the Victoria Cross for performing a heroic act which saved the lives of many of his fellow soldiers. On 10 June 1855, Lyons was amongst those seeking shelter during a Russian bombardment of the British trenches. When an unexploded shell landed beside him, Lyons quickly picked it up and threw it out of the trench. He had acted not a moment too soon, as the shell exploded seconds later. When Lyons died at Naas, County Kildare in April 1867, his relations dressed him in his uniform with his medals attached. Lyons looked so smart, they decided to prop him up in a chair and take a photograph.

❧

AN advert placed in the Belfast edition of the *Buy and Sell* magazine in February 1999 read: 'Gravestone, £250, would suit someone with the name Burns.'

❧

A copper beech at Coole Park, Gort, County Galway is called 'The Autograph Tree' because of the initials carved on its trunk by Lady Augusta Gregory and her guests – literary luminaries such as William Butler Yeats,

George Bernard Shaw and John Millington Synge. A protective metal railing now surrounds the tree to prevent other people from adding their initials.

THERE are several extraordinary exhibits on display in the Natural History Museum on Dublin's Merrion Square. One of the most unusual is a bird's nest that was discovered sealed inside a tree trunk by someone who was chopping it up for firewood. A card explains: 'The nest was made by a blue tit and was also used by a coal tit. A little later the tree must have grown in such a way as to completely close the hole, leaving portions of the eggs of both species in the nest.'

IN 1938 Kathleen ffrench bequeathed Monivea Castle in County Galway to the Irish nation as a home for indigent artists, but her wishes were ignored and her former home destroyed.

ON display in the Natural History Museum of Ireland is the eight-inch sword of a sailfish, which had pierced part of a ship's plank. The six-inch-thick section of timber with the sword still embedded in it shows how deadly a weapon the sailfish's blade was. Little appears to be known about the circumstances of this attack, the date or name of the vessel involved. All the exhibit's plaque records is that it was presented to the museum by Samuel R. Graves of Liverpool.

HOW many of the congregation of St Mark's on Pearse Street have ever climbed up into the belfry to view the bell that calls them to worship? It has hung there since 1761, when it was presented to the church. An inscription on it reads, ' the gift of Colonel Joshua Paul, 1761'. Around the upper part of the bell runs a curious verse of poetry:

> 'To the Church the living call,
> And to the Grave do summon all.'

∽

IN April 1946, the Finnerty family of Abbeygate Street, Galway made a surprising discovery when a much-loved picture they had owned for nearly 30 years dropped from the wall of their sitting room. A note fell out of the back of the picture, revealing its true provenance. The Finnertys had always assumed that it was just a simple, but beautiful black and white picture of a three-masted sailing vessel struggling in a stormy sea. In reality it was a candleograph made in 1875 by James Edmund Wood, 5 Queen Street, Plymouth. The note stated that the picture was done entirely with a candle and wick, and that no pencil or brush was used in its creation. The picture was full of detail and measured two feet by a foot and a half.

∽

ON 2 August 1865, a pyramid-shaped stone fell from the sky near Cashel, County Tipperary. In his *Report to the Royal Irish Academy*, Dr Haughton comments: 'A singular feature is observable in this stone, that I have never seen in any other: the rounded edges of the pyramid are sharply marked by lines on the black crust, as perfect as if made by a ruler.' Dr Haughton then speculated that the curious marks had been made by 'some peculiar tension in the cooling'.

&

IN June 1801, a mirage of an unknown city was seen for more than an hour at Youghal, County Cork. Onlookers described it as an aristocratic town of mansions set in shrubberies behind white palings. This was not the first time Youghal had experienced this phenomenon. In October 1796 another mirage of a walled town had been seen for over half an hour. Several months later, on 9 March 1797, a second mirage of a walled town appeared in Youghal.

&

RENVYLE Lough in County Galway is the sole recorded habitat of a rare water plant, *Hydrilla Verticillata*, which is extinct in Britain and unrecorded elsewhere in Ireland.

&

IN 1870, Ely Lodge near Enniskillen, County Fermanagh was blown up as part of the 21st birthday celebrations of the 4th Marquess of Ely, who intended to build a new house. It is also said that he blew up the house in order to avoid having Queen Victoria to stay. In any event, the new house was never built, because the young peer spent too much money on rebuilding his other seat, Loftus Hall in County Wexford.

&

AT 8.30 p.m. on 24 December 1909, James Fergusen of Rossbrien, County Limerick saw a luminous object appear above the north-eastern horizon and slowly move southwards. At 8.50 p.m. it turned around and retraced its path and disappeared at two minutes past nine.

※

ON 6 March 1896, John Brown of Dunmurry, Belfast imported the first car into Ireland. It was a Serpollet steam car from France. Sadly it was not a success, owing to the poor quality of Irish roads. As a result of his experiences with the Serpollet, Brown went on to become the founder member of the Irish Roads Improvement Association.

※

IRISHWOMAN Catherine Murphy was the last woman in Britain or Ireland to be executed by burning. She was executed on 18 March 1789 for the crime of counterfeiting money. Her three co-defendants, including her husband, were executed at the same time by hanging, but the law required that she be burnt at the stake. However, it was common practice to hang the woman for half an hour before setting her alight, and this was done. It is likely that Catherine Murphy was already dead before being set alight. Burning as a form of execution was abolished the following year.

※

SOMETIME during 1797 Colonel John Ogle walked 53 miles from Dublin to Dundalk in 10 hours, to win a bet of a penny!

※

MEN cutting turf near the banks of Cro-Leibhne Lake, Carrick, County Donegal in mid-May 1950 sighted a monster eel in the lake. They stated that it was over 15 feet long and eight feet in circumference. It had a remarkably large head. Three of the men saw the monster rising twice in the centre of the lake. A similar monster was reported to have been seen in the lake 50 years previously.

∽

IN the Melbourne *Australasian Medical Gazette* for January 1886, Dr Sinclair writes about the tragic and bizarre death of a 25-year-old Irishman. Crazed from habitual drunkenness, the youth cut off one testicle with a wire nail, then the other with a trouser-buckle. Even after these horrific injuries, he drove a nail into his own temple, first through the skin by striking it with his hand, and then by butting it against the wall – which caused his death.

∽

PEPPER'S Ghost is the name of an exhibit with a curious history in the Natural History Museum, Dublin. The fish was taken in the Doorosbeg-Mountcharles area of Lough Derg by District Inspector J.W. Pepper of the Royal Irish Constabulary on 1 September 1861. Weighing 13.8 kilograms, it was caught on a copper spool and took 50 minutes to play before being lifted from the water. For many years it was believed to be the largest trout ever caught in Ireland. Doubts were frequently expressed as to its authenticity. To clear the matter up, the specimen was scientifically examined by Dr A. E. J. Went of the Department of Fisheries in 1964. He carefully examined its scales and pronounced it to be a salmon.

⋰

WITH the disqualification of Pepper's Ghost from the record book, the title of the largest Irish trout went to a specimen taken from Lough Ennell, County Westmeath by William Meares on 15 August 1894. It weighed 11.8 kilograms when caught and still holds the record despite many challenges.

⋰

OVER a period of 170 years a total of 84 members of the Lynch family of Lynch's Castle in Galway were mayors of the city. Dominick solicited and procured the charter of Richard III in 1484. His brother Pierce became the first mayor of Galway. Dominick was the second. The last member of the family was Thomas FitzAmbrose Lynch, who was elected mayor of Galway in 1654. Later that year Cromwellian forces expelled Lynch. Lynch's Castle on the corner of Shop Street and Upper Abbey Street still stands.

⋰

HEARING the crash of breaking glass, Johanna Power of Kilrossanty, County Waterford investigated and found a dead hawk on the floor of her bedroom, with a dead bullfinch in its claws. A large mirror facing the open window was shattered by the force of the collision when the hawk dashed through the window on 9 February 1950.

⋰

AT an inquest held to investigate the death of a 14-year-old Wicklow boy, the coroner revealed that a dream resulted in the finding of the body of Patrick Burke, who had been missing for over a month. He had disappeared from his home in Rathdrum on 17 December 1928. Despite repeated searches by gardaí and neighbours along the nearby Avonmore River, his body was not discovered until 24 January 1929. It was found wedged between two boulders in the river, a mile from the dead boy's home. Since Patrick's disappearance, the river had been patrolled daily by the gardaí and other searchers, but had failed to locate the body. At the inquest a neighbour of the Burke family, Michael Hyland, testified that he had had a dream on the night of 23 January, in which he discovered the boy's body wedged between two rocks on the river at the place where the body was later found. Other neighbours verified that he related the strange dream to them the following morning. Hyland told the boy's father and both men went to the particular spot he had dreamt about. Patrick Burke, Sr. took off his boots and stockings, went into the river and searched with his hands between the two rocks. He felt a body, and lifted it up sufficiently to identify it as his son's. On medical evidence, the jury returned a verdict of 'death by accidental drowning'.

❧

NICHOLAS SIMPSON, of Cursed Stream, County Dublin, left a will in 1726 that pulled no punches. In somewhat strong language, he bequeaths his wife 'one shilling, and no more, because she has taken away a considerable sum of money and a great quantity of goods belonging to my house, and she has kept several strange men company, and hath remained out of my house sometimes one night, then several nights, and sometimes for six months together, and particularly with one Patrick Darling, who was a Papist and then a foot-soldier.'

∽

THE *Dublin Medical Press* for 1854 described an extraordinary suicide where a person had thrust a red-hot poker into his abdomen before pulling it out, causing fatal internal injuries.

∽

ON display in Dublin's famous Christ Church cathedral is a macabre exhibit. In the 1860s a cat and a rat (presumably the one chasing the other) were trapped in an organ pipe. Their mummified remains were later found and have been put on view ever since.

∽

NATTERJACK toads were probably introduced to Ireland since there are no ancient records or fossil remains. They could have come in ships' ballast collected abroad from coastal sand dunes in the days when sailors used this to stabilise their ships when they had no cargo on board. Natterjack toads were not known in Ireland before 1805 and are now found only in a small area of County Kerry. They are one of only three amphibians in Ireland – the others being the frog and the smooth newt. They are a protected species found only in areas of coastal sand dunes.

∽

JOHN COFFEE, who built the jail in Dundalk in 1853, went bankrupt on the project and was the first inmate of his own jail.

✧

UNTIL relatively recent times, large numbers of animals were a normal sight on the streets of every village, town and city in Ireland. Pigs let loose by their owners to scavenge for food on the streets were a particular nuisance and there are numerous records of attempts by the authorities to deal with this menace. Slane village in County Meath was no different in this regard. In 1788 the parish vestry ordered the village constable to shoot at sight all pigs found wandering through the village's streets. Apparently the constable did not carry out his orders ruthlessly enough and pigs on the streets were as numerous as ever six years later. On 22 April 1794 the vestry considered the problem again and came up with an imaginative solution to the problem. The meeting's minutes record their resolution: 'The constable has for the last year grossly neglected his duty in suffering pigs to range about the streets of this town to the great annoyance of the inhabitants and landowners of this parish. Resolved, therefore, that the said constable be fined the sum of five shillings for each pig seen ranging the streets from the day of the confirmation of this vestry; the fines to be levied off the goods of said constable by sale thereof, by warrant under the hand and seal of a magistrate, one half of the fine to be paid to the informer, and the other to the poor of this parish, and as an encouragement to the said constable he shall receive a premium of two shillings, the same to be paid by the church-wardens on producing the dead pigs.'

A foul-smelling substance, the consistency of butter, fell over large areas of southern Ireland in the winter and spring of 1696. According to the Bishop of Cloyne, this 'stinking dew' fell in 'lumps, often as big as the end of one's finger'. It was 'soft, clammy, and of a dark yellow colour'. The cattle in the fields where it fell continued to feed as usual. According to Mr Robert Vans of Kilkenny, the local people believed the 'butter' was a useful medicine and collected it in pots and pans.

ONE of the most remarkable creatures exhibited in the Natural History Museum of Ireland in Dublin is the black swallower (*Chiasmodon niger*). This deep-sea fish has the ability to capture and swallow other fish several times larger than itself. When the specimen on display was found floating on the surface of the ocean near Dominica in the West Indies in 1865, a specimen of *Scopelus macrolepidotus* was visible in its extended stomach. Its meal can still be clearly seen through the thin skin of its body. The black swallower is a luminous fish, and lures prey to it in the dark depths of the ocean using its own light. Just like a snake, its jaws are inde-pendent of each other. Once the black swallower seizes its prey, it hauls the victim into its stomach, one jaw moving forward, then the other. As the helpless captive is taken in, the swallower's stomach stretches until at last the entire fish is accommodated within it.

Sometimes its decomposing meal fills the swallower's stomach with gas, and it floats like a helpless balloon to the surface, which is how the museum's specimen was caught.

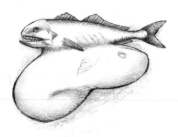

≪

IN January 1960, a Canadian beaver died peacefully in Dublin Zoo. However, during a post mortem examination, a curious anomaly was found. A small bullet, probably a .22, was embedded in its skull. The animal did not die from any cause associated with the bullet, though. Since it was impossible for the animal to have been shot in its den at Dublin Zoo, it seems most likely that it was shot in the Canadian wild, survived to be taken to Calgary Zoo, and then made the aeroplane journey to Dublin.

≪

MUCH has been written about Christian Cavanagh and Jennifer Hodgers, two Irish women who disguised themselves as men and went to war. But little is known about another Irish woman, Mary Storey, who also enjoyed life in the military in the 18th century. The records of the Royal Hospital in Kilmainham, Dublin preserve a reference to her. In March 1744 she was recommended to the board of governors as having served in the army and being deserving of their compassion. They agreed and ordered that 'she be allowed 18d. a week on the Out-pension from this day (1 March 1744).' Perhaps the life story of this extraordinary woman lies forgotten in a dusty archive? How many other Irish women went to war disguised as men and enjoyed a military career without ever being discovered?

⤚

ON 24 August 1895, a Donegal boy, Robert Alcorn, saw a large luminous object falling from the sky. It exploded near him. Alcorn put up his hands to shield his face. There was a second explosion, which shattered Alcorn's fingers. No remains of the object that had exploded were found.

⤚

IN October 1789 the following tale was published in a Dublin newspaper: 'On Monday night the people of a tavern in Essex Street were much surprised by the roaring of an animal under the kitchen. When raising some flags (beneath which the Poddle River runs) they discovered a fine young bull, which they then took up, and preserved its life for the owner, of whom they have yet heard nothing. It is not known how it got into the sewer, but it is supposed to have been swept down the Poddle hole.'

⤚

THE now obscure term 'Ardnacrusha rabbit' has its origins somewhere in the period from 1925 to 1929 when the massive hydroelectric scheme at Ardnacrusha on the river Shannon was under construction. Over 5,000 Irish and German workers toiled side by side on the scheme. Although they did not fraternise to any great extent, some men did form friendships. One German always ate rabbit pie for lunch, and every day he shared it with an Irish friend. 'By the way,' said the Irishman one lunch hour, 'where do you get your rabbits? I never see any around here.' 'Ach!' replied the German, 'I shoot zem. Every night zey make noise outside house and I shoot.' 'But rabbits don't make a noise,' said the Irishman cautiously. 'Zey go "meow, meow",' was the reply, and thus the 'Ardnacrusha rabbit' was born.

❧

ON 2 August 1908 a mirage of a faraway city was seen at Ballyconneely, on the Connemara coast. It was described as a city of different-sized houses, in different styles of architecture, and was visible for over three hours.

❧

THE etiquette which existed in the Royal Navy in the days of sailing ships caused senior officers to lead a very solitary life. This frequently affected their nerves, and their habits were often marked by an eccentricity bordering on madness. One such officer frequently moved a pig or donkey into his stateroom on the pretext that it reminded him of home. Another, a retired admiral who lived near Quilty, County Clare, was quite sane except for labouring under the unfortunate delusion that he was made of glass. When he moved about, the admiral fastened pillows around his person to serve as fenders. One day, awakened by a sudden noise, he rushed pillowless to the stairhead, slipped and fell. 'Broken, by Gad!' were his last words, as he reached the bottom and died.

⋘

IN February 1928 a lecture on the Shannon Hydroelectric power scheme was held in Dublin. Owing to a mishap, it was a disaster. It was to have been illustrated by slides, but the machine broke down after a few minutes and all attempts to resurrect it failed. This does not say much for the skills of those attending the meeting because they were all electrical engineers! After the efforts of half a dozen electrical engineers failed to correct the fault, the meeting adjourned.

⋘

JOHN CHANDLER earned fame of a kind on 16 January 1950, when he landed in Halifax, Nova Scotia, after making his third involuntary transatlantic crossing in 20 years, because storms prevented him from leaving the ship. Piloting the Cunard liner *Franconia*, out of Cobh Harbour, Chandler found himself stormbound and was forced to remain on the liner while she crossed the Atlantic. He had a similar experience in 1940 when he landed in Halifax. Before that, he ended up in New York in 1930 on his first forced passage. It is not recorded if Chandler made any more involuntary crossings of the Atlantic.

⋘

IRELAND'S most bizarre and least-known mystery is that of the Chinese seals. Since 1780 over 60 small porcelain seals (inscribed stamps) have been discovered throughout Ireland in obscure places such as riverbeds, peat bogs, caves, tillage fields and under the roots of trees. Charles Fort, the famous American collector of all things strange and unexplained, was intrigued by the mystery and studied it at length, but could not shed any light on it.

The seals are tiny, consisting of a cube measuring about one inch, surmounted by the figure of an animal, and are made of a special type of hard porcelain known as *blanc de chine*. Such seals were made for Chinese scholars, who would have owned 20 or 30 of them. Each seal bore an auspicious message and the scholar would have used the most appropriate one to seal his letter. They were common in the East but unknown in Europe. What were they doing in Ireland, especially when such seals were never discovered in similar circumstances anywhere else in Europe? In the decades following their discovery, the mystery of the Chinese seals stirred fierce debate among Irish antiquarians, but the mystery was never solved. In the early 1980s, at prophetic science-fiction writer Arthur C. Clarke's request, Jan Chapman, an Oriental expert from Dublin's Chester Beatty Library, examined some of the seals on display in the National Museum of Ireland. She was able to identify the porcelain as a product of a factory near one of China's main trading ports, Amoy. Chapman concluded that the seals found in Ireland dated from the early 18th century, but beyond that the origins of the Chinese seals remain as puzzling as they were over two centuries ago.

ONE of the few white men to witness a cannibal feast – and live to tell about it – was Dubliner Terence McGovern, who attended one on the Solomon Islands in the sultry South Seas around the end of the 19th century. He was revolted by what he saw and could not bring himself to taste the human flesh on offer, even though he risked offending his hosts.

❧

ABOUT four o'clock on the afternoon of 18 June 1748 a ferocious thunderstorm hit Cork City. Hailstones, some measuring five inches in diameter, pummelled the city, breaking windows and causing considerable damage.

❧

ONE of the most curious items collected by 70-year-old Billy Dunbar from Newtownstewart, County Tyrone is a threepenny bit engraved with the Lord's Prayer. He sold most of his eclectic collection to Strabane District Council in 2000 (it is now held at Gray's Printing Museum in Strabane), but the three-penny bit was given to a family member.

❧

ON 13 November 1953, Martin Nee from Inverin, Co. Galway, who was serving with the British Army in Berlin, defected to East Germany. A statement from the communist government quoted Nee as saying that he wanted to do all he could to prevent a third world war: 'That is why I have come here.'

❧

A Pieyel piano owned by the Columban Fathers of Navan, County Meath is one of three remaining in the world. Only four were made in 1880. The instrument is Siamese and has a keyboard at both ends.

⚜

IN the 1860s a foreign vessel was pounded to pieces on the rocks near Balscadden Bay near Howth. One of the crew was washed ashore and taken to St Michael's Hospital in Dun Laoghaire on account of his terrible injuries. His situation was so bad that doctors despaired and a priest was brought in to hear his confession and dying words. The unfortunate man had only a few words of English. Otherwise he spoke in a strange language that was unknown to any linguists brought in to try and communicate with him. No one could understand a word he said. Oscar Wilde's father, Sir William, who was visiting physician to the hospital, got a sudden inspiration and rushed off to fetch his wife. When Lady Wilde was brought to the sailor's bedside, she spoke to him, and the man turned to her with a look of delight and answered her. The other bystanders withdrew and left Lady Wilde to interpret the dying man's confession to the hospital chaplain. How had Sir William Wilde known that his wife would be able to communicate with the man when others had failed? He guessed that the dying man was a Basque, whose language is totally different to all other European languages. Lady Wilde had learned the language from a much-loved Basque nurse in her childhood and was one of the very small number of people – if not the only Irish person – who spoke the language at that time. A

124

lucky guess and incredible coincidence meant that the unfortunate sailor far from home died, comforted by another Basque speaker.

❧

WHEN Kennys of Galway launched their website in 1993, they were only the second bookshop in the world to do so. The first bookseller to have a website was a crime fiction bookshop in San Francisco.

❧

IN 1829, the year of Catholic Emancipation, a strange custom was terminated at St Audoen's Church in Dublin. Until then it had been the custom to the toll the church bells annually on 22 October at midnight to commemorate the capture of Lord Conor Maguire, arrested that night in the year 1641 at the house of one Kerne, 'a Taylor', in Cook Street, and charged with conspiracy. Maguire was executed some years later at Tyburn in London. For nearly 200 years an annual daytime service and night-time bell-ringing celebrated his capture.

❧

ON 2 October 2005 at Elm Green Golf Club, Castleknock, Dublin, Ronan Quinlan and his golfing partner Brendan Quinn accidentally killed two birds – a robin and a seagull – during a round of golf. The tragic fluke events occurred as follows: on the 13th hole, Quinn hit a 6 iron second shot from about 160 yards. The ball hit a flying robin and decapitated the poor bird. On the 16th hole, Quinlan hit a second shot, a 3 wood, and hit a flying seagull, which instantly dropped to the fairway, stone dead. In both cases the birds were flying alone.

~

THE heaviest ever Irishman is said to have been Roger Byrne (1750–1804) from Rosenallis, County Laois. When he was buried on 14 March 1804 his coffin and its contents weighed a staggering 52 stone (330 kg). Another Irish heavyweight was the splendidly named Lovelace Love (1731–66) from Brook Hill, Co. Mayo. He reputedly weighed over 40 stone (254 kg) at the time of his death.

~

CAPTAIN J.B. Drought dedicated his 1937 book, *Green Memory of Days with Gun and Rod*, to 'The best bag I ever made in Ireland – my wife'.

~

IN May 1997, Joseph Peterson, aged 47, from Belfast, fell 150 feet (46 m) off a cliff, breaking both legs and an arm. He had stopped to pick a four-leaf clover on a hilltop while on holiday near Lake Como in Italy.

~

ECCENTRIC genius Richard Kirwan (1733–1812) harboured an obsessive hatred of flies. He despised them so much that he paid his servants a bounty on each dead fly they produced.

~

A more recent case of battling birds occurred in November 1930 – also in County Cork. Several hundred rooks and a few jackdaws nested in two groups of tall trees, one in Fermoy and one on an island in the Blackwater River, below Fermoy bridge. In a pine wood about a mile and a half away, there was a huge roost of some 10,000–12,000 starlings. On 2 November, after the rooks had retired for the evening, an enormous flock of starlings started wheeling round and round the town for a while, then suddenly poured into the rooks' nesting places. The rooks took to the skies and protested noisily but the starlings refused to budge. The outnumbered rooks had to camp elsewhere. Each night for a week the same fracas occurred, but on 9 November there was a surprise in store for the starlings. Instead of facing the usual 300 or so rooks, a black mass of anything between 1,500 and 2,000 rooks rose up to repel the invaders, cawing noisily. They did not attack the starlings, but 'hovered densely packed' a few feet above the tree tops. Four times the starlings poured down, but each time the rooks rose up and warded them off. In the end most of the starlings admitted defeat and went back to their own pine wood, but a small group of determined birds evaded the rooks and held their ground until 11 November, when they were finally driven off by the same tactics. The rooks remained in force until 14 November, then the garrison was gradually reduced until the population returned to its normal level. The starlings never made another attempt to take the rooks' territory, and eventually left the area. It was a remarkable achievement by the rooks and a stunning display of organisation on their part. They won the 'battle' without a single act of violence, after they had summoned reinforcements and outmanoeuvred the starlings without a blow being struck.

❦

127

JOHN 'CAPTAIN JACK' TONER (c. 1867–1929) from Blackhill, County Tyrone lived an adventurous life. He sailed around the world on various tramp steamers, fought in the Boer War, worked on the Panama Canal excavations, prospected for gold in the frozen Alaskan wilderness and endured the harsh life of a hunter and fur trapper in the Arctic regions of Canada. It is not surprising that by 1916 Toner decided that there were easier ways of making a living.

He decided to start a restaurant – not a fashionable premises in a city with waiters and menus, but a rough and ready eatery in the heart of the Canadian wilderness. With an axe, a hammer, some cooking pots and a sheet-iron stove, Tonner settled in Cow Bay, Prince Rupert's Land, British Columbia. Here, with his own hands, he constructed a sort of floating restaurant and home and catered for a clientele of trappers and fishermen. It was best described as a floating shack – a kind of Noah's Ark, inhabited by dogs, fish, clam and crabs and, strangest of all, John Toner himself. It quickly became a *rendez vous* for his fishermen cronies. The Ark and its owner were described in Lowell Thomas's *The First World Flight*, a book about the planes which flew around the world in 1924. They stopped off at Prince Rupert's Land, where Toner was on hand to look after the men and guard their machines. Before the aviators left, Toner had them autograph his front door, then proudly had the door photographed and varnished to preserve their autographs as a souvenir. Toner's neighbours were envious, and when he went fishing one day he returned to find that someone had stolen his front door!

∾

IN the 1740s and 1750s an imbecilic Irishman became famous in London for his capacity to eat great amounts of raw meat. According to the newspapers of the time, Dublin man Thomas Eclin was 'remarkable for his vivacity and drollery in the low way.' His feats included eating live dogs and cats and leaping head first into the Thames when the weather was freezing cold. Eclin was very fond of drinking copious amounts of gin, and after his death from vomiting blood, the *Daily Advertiser* announced the sale of a drawing in his honour, depicting the cat eater with the 'just emblems of his ambition: a decanter and a glass at his elbow, and a pipe in his right hand.'

THERE are many stories of dogs and cats travelling long distances to the home of their choice. A friend of the former *Irish Times* editor Robert Smyllie (1894–1954) was very fond of his cat. He hated the idea of leaving it behind to be looked after by neighbours, or being lodged in a cattery, so he decided to take it with him on holiday. He brought him with him in a basket and travelled from Dublin to County Tipperary. All was well for about four days, and then the cat went missing. The owner spent most of the rest of his holiday searching for his beloved cat, before reluctantly coming to the conclusion that the cat had been killed by dogs. Ten days after the cat had gone missing, its owner returned home. When he opened the hall door, the first thing to greet him was a plaintive meow from his rather emaciated cat.

DURING the seventeenth century, Belfast Church authorities hired out cloaks for funerals. The price ranged from one shilling to 15 shillings, according to quality. The number of cloaks worn by mourners indicated the social position of the deceased.

๛

IN August 1929, a curious epitaph was discovered on a wall by builders working on bank premises at the Diamond in Coleraine, County Derry. The epitaph was written to commemorate the loss by fire in 1863 of the pair-oared racing boat, *The Gazelle*, belonging to the famous Bann Rowing Club. It was in a perfect state of preservation, although written with a black lead pencil 66 years previously. In scroll form, surmounted by cup and cross, the epitaph reads: '*Requiescat in pace*: Sacred to the memory of *The Gazelle*. This monument is erected by its surviving friends as a memento of that beautiful and fast-racing gig, which was burned on the date below, at two o'clock a.m. It carried many a fair and noble crew, amongst whom we may mention our beautiful coxwain, whose presence often graced the departed boat, and whose smiles beguiled many a long row, and to whom stroke and bow take this opportunity of returning their heartfelt thanks for the gallant and unsurpassable manner in which he steered that noble boat (Memento Mori). We sorrowing, but not without hope that the Road Sessions will give us compensation and wipe away our tears with heavy damages, and that again a boat will be wafted along, steered by that fair and adorable coxwain and rowed by that manly crew subscribe our names this 7th day of July, in the year of our Lord 1863 – H.A. Macaulay, B.W. Thompson, M.A. Macaulay.'

৯

REVEREND Daniel Lysons's *Collecteana,* scrapbooks of newspaper clippings and handbills and advertisements detailing the colourful side of 18th-century London, is a vast source of cultural history. It is carefully kept among the vast manuscript collections of the British Library in London. Among the most startling items pasted into the scrapbooks are a collection of articles and letters regarding an unsavoury bet by an Irish rake Richard Barry, 7th Earl of Barrymore from County Cork. On 13 March 1788 the following item appeared in *The World*: 'Amongst the curious Betts of the day, may be reckoned the following: The Duke of Bedford has betted 1000 guineas with Lord Barrymore, that he does not – *eat a live Cat*! It is said his Lordship grounds his chances upon having already made the experiment upon a Kitten. The Cat is to be fed as Lord Barrymore may choose.' This unusual bet attracted considerable public attention and several letters and articles appeared in subsequent issues of *The World* under the heading 'Cat Eating.' Barrymore was a notorious rake who had wasted his health and fortune gambling and whoring away to his heart's content. He later wrote to the newspaper to say its report had been mistaken; he had bet only that he could find 'a man who would eat a cat'. But despite this disclaimer, letters from self-appointed experts on competitive eating continued to get into print. One of these had, in 1777, seen an Irishman eat five fox cubs on a bet of 50 pounds at a racecourse near Kildare and observed that 'the bet of his Grace of Bedford, that Lord Barrymore will not eat a live cat, is not without precedents in the annals of sporting.'

⚜

THE Royal Marriage Act, which gives the British monarch the final say over whom members of their family might marry, was added to the English statute book because of an Irish woman. In the 18th and 19th centuries many notable Irishwomen were famous for their ability to make the most of their beauty and wit and snare a wealthy husband. For example, Elizabeth Gunning from Roscommon captured two dukes in succession (in time, four of her sons from these marriages became dukes), but Anne Luttrell of Luttrellstown Castle in Dublin went one better: she landed no less a personage than H.R.H. the Duke of Cumberland, brother of King George III. Anne had married young to Christopher Horton, a Derbyshire squire, who considerately died and left her a widow at the age of 24. According to the diarist Horace Walpole, she was 'extremely pretty…a coquette beyond measure and as artful as Cleopatra…with eyelashes a yard long.' The Duke of Cumberland was weak-minded and easily led. He soon found he was no match for the beautiful widow. Before he knew where he was, he had eloped with her to Calais, where they secretly married in October 1771. Once married, the artful adventuress had no wish to spend her life in exile in France. She was a Royal Duchess now and determined that the world should know it. The couple returned to England and broke the news to the King. He was furious and swore that 'that woman should never become a Royal Duchess'. The Duchess of Cumberland was banned from court and ostracised by high society.

More importantly, the King acted to prevent future unsuitable alliances from being contracted by the royal family. To this end, the Royal Marriage Act was introduced in February 1772, ensuring that no member of the royal family could marry without the monarch's consent. Nevertheless, what was done could not be undone. Anne Luttrell was legally Duchess of Cumberland – she had been clever enough to see to that. It is also true that she did not gain much by her scheming because the King and Queen and high society all snubbed her. She endured the insult in dignified silence and waited patiently for an opportunity to take her revenge. When it came at last, the Cumberlands did not hesitate to act. At this time the young Prince of Wales was the nation's bright young hope, and a very different individual from the person who lived to rule a disillusioned people as George IV. With merciless ingenuity, the Duke and Duchess frequently invited the young Prince to their home and made it easy for him to drink and gamble. In no time at all he was part of the London fast set, gambling, drinking and womanising with other young rakes. To the King and Queen's despair, the Cumberlands had had their revenge. Eventually the Prince persuaded his parents to receive the Duchess and she was finally admitted to the ranks of high society.

❦

BECAUSE his pride would not allow him to beg for food, 49-year-old unemployed Irish emigrant Dominic Nolan starved to death rather than ask for handouts. In late July 1928 the Irishman's remains were found in dense scrub near Auckland, New Zealand. As he lay starving, Nolan had written letters warning emigrants to stay in their homeland and not to travel 'Down Under'. Nolan had emigrated to New Zealand three years before and had been able to find only sporadic employment. He blamed the British government, who, anxious to rid Britain and Ireland of some of their unemployed, used dazzling advertisements portraying the Antipodes as a wealthy paradise crying out for workers. In fact, these countries were in deep economic depression, and many native citizens had been out of work for years.

IN February 2002 a lamb with four ears was born on a farm in Summerhill, County Meath. Dolby, as the media called her, became a national celebrity. She was one of a set of twins born on a farm owned by the Corcoran family. Dolby's owner, Paul Corcoran, said that he had not noticed anything unusual when the lambs were born. It was only when Paul took a closer look that he realised that one of them had four ears. Three of the ears were on one side of Dolby's head, and

she had one ear on the other side. The unusual lamb with surround sound lived out the rest of her life in the lush fields of County Meath unfazed by the attention.

꼉

IN the 1860s, pranksters in Parkgate, County Antrim pulled off an audacious hoax on unsuspecting locals. All around the area posters suddenly appeared announcing a 'Cat Fair'. They read: 'I will attend at the Court House in Parkgate on the 7th February, to Purchase Cats for the Peruvian Government. From 10 to 20 shillings Each will be given according to size, Colour and Quality.' Mention of the Court House gave the advertisement the ring of truth and greed tempted thrifty housewives for miles around to collect and feed all the feline beauties they could lay their hands on. Scores of ordinarily shrewd women walked or drove into Parkgate on the morning of the fair with carefully tended cats in baskets and crates. As hour after hour passed, and no representative of the Peruvian government showed up, the housewives realised they had been fooled. Hundreds of cats, of all ages, sizes, colours and condition, were let loose through Parkgate. Old people who remembered this 'Cat Fair' many years later always said that never before or after had there been such a 'clatter' in Parkgate as on that day. The housewives' husbands later discovered that four local jokers had perpetrated the hoax. Shortly afterwards, one of them, a blacksmith named Aitchison, was paid back in kind. On his wedding night Aitchinson found himself and his bride locked and barricaded into their cottage. The purpose of this 'penning' became painfully obvious when a large basket of infuriated cats was lowered down the chimney. The din they made was worse than the 'Cat Fair' itself.

❧

JACK LANGAN (1798–1846) was a famous Dublin bare-knuckle boxer. In one of his early fights, Langan hit an opponent called Savage so hard that it was thought he had killed him. The unfortunate Savage was carried home, where his corpse was washed and laid out for a wake. At some stage during the proceedings, the house was cleared very rapidly when the corpse sat up abruptly, demanding to know what had happened to him.

❧

JUST as astrology and fortune-telling is now, it was a highly profitable and extremely competitive business in the early 18th century. Dublin astrologers never passed up an opportunity to discredit their rivals. Isaac Butler's main rival was an astrologist named La Boissière. In his almanac, *A Voice from the Stars*, Butler set out to discredit his opponent. He published a chart for La Boisière, using his birth date and the positioning of the stars and planets, and predicted that La Boissière would die on a certain day. Unfortunately for Butler, La Boissière survived, but on the very day in question, Butler's own father was knocked down and killed by a horse and cart! In the next issue of his own almanac, La Boissière asked Butler why he had not predicted his father's death and tried to prevent it.

❧

WHEN Lieutenant Charles Wilkes of the U.S. Exploring Expedition of 1838–42 stepped ashore on one of the Fiji Islands during the fleet's heroic quest to map the entire Pacific Ocean, he was accosted by a man whom he first took to be a Fijian. In fact the man turned out to be a deeply tanned former sailor, Paddy O'Connell, originally from County Clare. Paddy had been living in Fiji for more than 40 years. He proudly told Wilkes that he had fathered 48 children and hoped to reach an even 50 before he died!

≼

W.J. HAMILTON, a lighthouse keeper stationed at Skellig lighthouse off the Kerry coast in the 1930s, made his own false teeth from the ivory handles of knives.

≼

THERE was little love lost between James Annesley (1715–66) and his wicked Uncle Richard. Annesley was the son and heir of wealthy Wexford landowner Arthur Annesley, fourth Baron Altham. After his mother died, a new mistress turned his father against him. The 10-year-old boy was thrown out on the streets of Dublin to survive on the charity of sympathetic souls. There was no one to press James's claims to his inheritance when his father died in 1727, so the title and estates passed to his father's younger brother, Richard, who was just as bad a rogue. James's uncle saw the boy as a threat, so he dealt with him ruthlessly. He had the 12-year-old boy kidnapped and sold into slavery in America, turning a profit on this cruel transaction. Thirteen years later,

James escaped and joined the Navy to secure passage home to claim his rightful inheritance. After an unprecedented 15-day court trial, judgment went to James. All he had to do was to present his claim to the House of Lords. Unfortunately, he was not able to raise the money and he died a year later, aged 45, worn out by the bitter struggle to reclaim his inheritance. The 'Annesley Claimant' case, as it was known, was famous in its day and inspired many novelists, including Sir Walter Scott and, most notably, Robert Louis Stevenson in *Kidnapped*.

❧

DUBLIN doctor Sir Charles Cameron (1830–1921) is one of the city's unsung heroes. He worked tirelessly to improve living conditions and sanitation in the nation's capital, helping reduce the mortality rate in Dublin, which was once the highest in Europe. In 1911 he was behind a bizarre scheme to rid the city of its houseflies, which had become a menace in that year's sweltering summer. Cameron's scheme offered threepence for every bag of dead flies presented to the cleansing depot at Marrowbone Lane. The scheme never caught on, probably because of the size of paper bags supplied by Dublin Corporation. It was estimated that it would take at least 6,000 flies to fill a bag! Cameron's fly extermination campaign was a great source of humour to Dubliners. It may have been an eccentric enterprise, but Cameron was no fool, and the city is forever in his debt.

❧

THE most sensational event in Trinity College, Dublin history occurred in 1734, when students murdered one of the Fellows. The Junior Dean, Edward Ford, was very unpopular with the undergraduates. One day he received warning that the windows of his rooms would be broken. That evening students showed up and proceeded to throw stones, but Ford was lying in wait for them with a gun at the ready and a large supply of ammunition. He fired down into them, enraging the students, who ran away and found a gun. In the following gunfight Ford was fatally wounded. Public opinion was on the students' side and Ford's actions were condemned! His killers received only a light punishment because many of those involved with the killing were from influential families.

≪

IN 1923, Oliver St John Gogarty (1878–1957), the writer, wit and surgeon, became a member of the first Free State Senate. He survived a republican kidnapping attempt by jumping into the river Liffey and swimming to freedom. In a typically theatrical gesture, Gogarty later celebrated his escape by presenting two swans to the 'spirit of the river'. The ceremony did not go according to plan. The two swans refused to leave their box until Gogarty kicked them out. Then, unlike their benefactor, they proved to be camera-shy. The official photograph of the occasion shows Gogarty and two very superimposed look-alike swans pasted on to replace the camera-shy originals. Dublin wits remarked that the swans had refused to be associated with such an amateur publicity stunt.

≪

HOW did Jonathan Swift know about the moons of Mars 150 years before they were discovered? Swift's

Gulliver's Travels is rightly considered to be a classic of world literature. Few people realise that it is also remembered for a strange prophecy made by Dean Swift concerning the red planet. First published in 1726, *Gulliver's Travels* contains the following remarkable passage in the 'Voyage to Laputa' section: 'Certain astronomers...have likewise discovered two lesser Stars, or Satellites, which revolve about *Mars*; whereof the innermost is distant from the Center of the primary Planet exactly three of his Diameters, and the outermost five; the former revolves in the space of ten Hours, and the latter in Twenty-one and a Half; so that the Squares of their periodical Times, are very near the same Proportion with the Cubes of their Distance from the Center of *Mars*.' At that time Mars was supposed to be without moons. A century and a half later, in 1877, an American astronomer, Asaph Hall, first sighted the two small moons orbiting Mars, which he named Phobos and Delmos. Amazingly, Swift was right about more than just the number of moons orbiting the planet. He also correctly placed them near to the planet and gave quite a close estimate of the amount of time it took each to revolve around Mars.

※

THE *Annual Register* (a chronicle of British and world history) for 1760 reported the death of 117-year-old James MacDonald at his home near Cork City. He had the unique double distinction of being extremely long-lived and being exceptionally tall. He was reputed to have been 7 ft 6 in at his prime. As a young man, MacDonald made his living as a touring giant. He became disillusioned at this vagabond way of life in

1685 and joined the British Army, serving as a grenadier for several years. MacDonald returned to Ireland in 1716 and settled in his native county, working as a labourer until just three years before his death.

৵

LORD Dunraven from Limerick (1841–1926) was a noted war correspondent and the only man who attended both the convention of Versailles, which ended the Franco-Prussian War in 1871, and the Treaty of Versailles, which ended World War I in 1919.

৵

AN amateur ventriloquist inadvertently caused panic on the streets of Dublin in 1832. Nearly 200 years later it still remains the most audacious hoax ever committed in the city. Before his death in 1877, the perpetrator, a Dr Seward, left an account of the chaos which ensued that fateful day.

> In 1832, on a wet December evening, I was return-ing from the College of Surgeons, accompanied by Samuel Bennet and George Burke. Passing Bridgefoot Street, opposite St Catherine's Church Bennet said, 'Come, Seward, give us a touch of your ventriloquism in that sewer there.' I complied, but did not intend that anyone but the two should hear me. I called from the sewer as if there was a person anxious to get out, saying he had made his way there from the Debtors' prison adjacent, that he was very weak, and must shortly die if not released. At the corner was an apple-woman's stall, who heard the dialogue from the sewer. We left at once, and heard her calling lustily for help. This

happened about five o'clock p.m. The postman called at my place to deliver a letter at six. 'Oh, sir,' said he, 'there's desperate work in Thomas Street: the prisoners have escaped from the Marshalsea, and they are digging them out of the sewer in the street.' It was raining very hard, and I ran down to the place. There was a large crowd, some with umbrellas, holding lighted lanterns, and men working for their very life with spades and picks, ripping up the sewer down Dirty Lane. I ran across Thomas Street to a grating near St Catherine's Church, and threw my voice into that opening. A person passing was attracted by the voice, and at once called out that he heard the man there. The operations continued with undiminished activity. That grating was at once torn up, and the street ripped open from one side to the other, stopping all traffic, then a great inconvenience, as Thomas Street was the leading thoroughfare to the south for the mail coaches, and all of which were obliged to go by Usher's Island instead. The news was all over Dublin in the morning, and I was received at the College as a hero – students flocking round me, and begging of me to speak in all quarters.

≪

IN 1220 the Priory of All Hallows (where Trinity College now stands) founded a hospice on nearby lands adjacent to the river Liffey for the use of lepers. According to one writer, the lepers were not allowed out of the grounds of the hospice unless they were accompanied by two attendants, one carrying a bell and crying out 'Unclean! Unclean!', the other carrying a 40-foot pole to keep 'clean' Dubliners out of the way.

≪

SAMUEL BOYCE (1708–49) was an eccentric Dublin poet who was famous for his lack of gratitude to patrons who could have saved him from poverty. After writing an elegy lamenting the death of Viscountess Stormount, he was offered a lucrative position in the customs by her husband. Since the day fixed for securing the appointment was rainy, Boyce preferred to lose the job rather than get wet. This and many other examples of his perverse ingratitude alienated Boyce from friends and patrons alike. When he died in abject poverty, no one would pay for his funeral, so he was buried like the pauper he was and was mourned by few.

❧

LIKE her younger sister Elizabeth, Maria Gunning (1734–60) from County Roscommon was a famous beauty of her day and escaped her humble origins by marrying into high society. When the sisters came of age, they turned to acting to make a living. In 1751 the Gunning sisters travelled to London to seek their fortune. They starred in many West End shows and quickly became celebrities. After a year Elizabeth married the Duke of Hamilton, while Maria married the Earl of Coventry. Maria was so famous and beautiful that she was mobbed by crowds of admirers whenever she appeared in public. As protection against being mobbed, King George II assigned her a permanent guard. Whenever Maria went out, she was always accompanied by six soldiers marching ahead to push aside the crowd, while another 12 with two sergeants followed close behind. King George II said: 'If necessary, I will devote the entire British Army to protect the most beautiful woman in the land.'

❧

IN the early 18th century, Elizabeth St Leger was initiated as one of the few women Freemasons in history, after she had been caught spying on a Lodge meeting held by her father, Arthur 1st Viscount Doneraile, at their home, Doneraile Court in County Cork.

❧

IN the late 18th century, the triumphal arch at the entrance to the demesne of Glananea, near Killucan, County Westmeath, was so grand that the owner, Smyth, came to be known as 'Smyth of the gates'. He quickly grew tired of the nickname and sold the arch to a neighbour of his at Rosmead near Delvin. To his annoyance, he now became known as 'Smyth without the gates'. Although Rosmead is now a ruin, the famous triumphal arch still proudly guards the entrance. In his *Guide to Irish Country Houses*, Mark Bence-Jones describes it as 'an elegant triumphal arch with Corinthian pilasters and large urns on the flanking walls'.

❧

ACCORDING to legend, anyone spanning the Cross of Cashel, at the Rock of Cashel, County Tipperary, where St Patrick is said to have baptised King Aengus in the fifth century, will become immune from toothache.

❧

IN October 2001, Bill 'Stretch' Coleman from Denver, Colorado, walked the Dublin Marathon while wearing stilts in a time of 8 hours, 53 minutes, 12 seconds, beating his previous record by one and a half hours.

❧

IN January 1996 an eight-month-old West Highland terrier from Belfast – a male dog, despite being called Zoë – became very newsworthy. The terrier earned a place in newspapers and veterinary journals because it was emitting a persistent humming noise from its ears. This rare phenomenon had occurred in a Welsh pony the previous year. Zoë's owner, Raymond Burrows, had first noticed the sound the previous November. The British Veterinary Association said that whistling ear syndrome (or 'otocoustic emisson') is similar to reverse tinnitus. There is no known cure, but most of the time the affected animals do not seem to be bothered by it. There is also a chance that the condition might resolve itself spontaneously.

DURING the American Civil War, Irishman Albert D.J. Cashier (1843–1915) enlisted in the Union Army. For the next three years he fought bravely in more than 40 battles. After the war, Cashier lived an uneventful life until 1911, when the 68-year-old was hit by a car and suffered a broken leg. The doctor treating him was astonished to discover that 'Albert' was actually a woman, but he kept her secret on condition that she stay in the Illinois State Veterans' Hospital. Two years later her secret came out and state officials sent her to a mental hospital, convinced that she was delusional for believing she was Albert Cashier. Her claim was verified after the federal government's Pension Bureau launched an investigation to see if she was entitled to the pension she had been claiming since 1890. In truth 'Albert' was Jennifer Hodgers from Clogherhead, County Louth, who had emigrated to America at an early age and went to war disguised as a man at the age of 21. After careful review of the evidence and interviews with dozens of Hodgers's fellow soldiers, it was confirmed that Hodgers and Cashier were one and the same and so the pension was maintained. She lived another 18 months at the hospital and died on 10 October 1915. Hodgers was buried in her army uniform and awarded full military honours.

৯

ALTHOUGH the custom might seem bizarre and perhaps gruesome to present-day sensibilities, funeral invitation cards were a highly fashionable accessory in the 18th century. They seem to have been widely used by the well-to-do of the time. One prime example existed at least into the 1930s. It was an invitation to attend the funeral of Sir Arthur Shaen, Bart, who died in 1725.

The illustrations and portions of the invitation are printed, but the personal names, the date and the places are hand-written, showing that this card was for general use, and not one specially printed for the occasion. King Death dominates, crowned upon a globe, with a dart in his right hand. Other emblems depicted are a pair of cross-bones, several skulls and an open hearse, with a canopy, drawn by six horses, plumed and mantled. Behind the hearse is an open coffin, showing a corpse in an elaborate funeral shroud. The designer of this wonderful oddity has clearly done full justice to Death and its trappings.

৯

TWO of the most bizarre treasures of Ireland's Natural History Museum are the kamikaze eels, which are tucked away in a corner on the ground floor, preserved in formaldehyde-filled glass jar coffins. One choked in an attempt to swallow a frog – the unfortunate creature's legs can still be seen protruding from the eel's mouth. J. W. Jackson of Enniscorthy, County Wexford presented it to the museum in 1929. The other specimen was choked by a smaller eel. Its victim's tail worked its way out through the eel's gill opening, thereby causing its suffocation. These eels were presented to the museum in 1932 by D. Quinlan of Rathflesk, Killarney, County Kerry.

WHAT is said to be the least successful pigeon race of all time occurred in 1983, when the Northern Ireland Pigeon Racing Society lost 16,430 birds in one go. Although a handful of the duller birds flew straight home in record time, swarms of the more adventurous little creatures were later found basking in country gardens all over west Wales. Housewives were asked to leave out rice, lentils and dried peas to keep up their strength. Eventually, special transport was laid on for their journey home.

IRELAND'S tallest woman is reputedly Mary Murphy from Portrush, County Antrim, who stood an incredible 7 ft 2 in, without shoes or headgear. She was very beautiful and had no shortage of suitors. She turned them all down and married a French sea captain who happened to be passing through the port of Portrush. Her husband retired from the sea and together they toured France and Britain, with Mary appearing as the 'celebrated giantess' in her own special private show. In 1689, aged 23, she appeared in a sideshow in Portrush and at an exhibition in Fleet Street, London. During the 1690s she went to London, where she visited the court of King William III and Queen Mary. She danced an Irish jig and sang an Irish song, for which she was paid a fee of one guinea. Mary's last recorded appearance was at a fair at Montpellier in Languedoc, France in 1701. By that time she had been abandoned by her husband and was destitute.

ON 27 January 1746 a family in Kilmoloda parish in East Carbery, County Cork were hit by lightning while they slept. Robert Barry, his wife and two children were asleep in their bed when lightning hit the cottage's chimney, damaging it, then struck their bedroom door, which was shut, with such force that it demolished it. Robert Barry and his family suffered burn injuries from the encounter. Barry's shoulder and chest were burnt, while the side of the face that his wife lay on was very swollen and painful. Their daughter had her hair burnt close to her temples, and their son was scorched on the back of his neck. As unlucky as they had been, they were

fortunate to escape with their lives; outside a dead pig was found near the chimney. The family did not know what had happened to them until neighbours came at daybreak to see if they were all right. They all recovered from their ordeal. Incidentally, Robert Barry reported finding a stone on his chest when he woke up.

≪

IN the 18th century, an Englishman who had always hated the Irish inherited a property in County Tipperary, on condition he resided there. He had no choice but to agree to this distasteful (to him) condition, but when he died on 17 March 1791, his will revealed how he wished to take his revenge. He left an annual sum of 10 pounds for the purchase of a large quantity of whiskey, to be distributed among not more than 20 Irishmen who were to assemble in the graveyard where he was buried, on every anniversary of his death. The whiskey was to be served in half-pint measures and each Irishman was to be provided with a stout oaken stick and a knife. His will concluded: 'Knowing what I know of the Irish character, my conviction is, that these materials given, they will not fail to destroy each other, and when in the course of time the race comes to be exterminated, this neighbourhood at least may perhaps, be colonised by civilised and respectable Englishmen.'

≪

THE strange saga of John MacNaughten of Benvarden, Devock, County Antrim is still remembered today because of the manner of his death. In November 1761 MacNaughten accidentally shot dead wealthy heiress Mary Anne Knox of Preben while attempting to abduct her. (He was aiming at her father.) MacNaughten was quickly captured, tried, sentenced to death and hanged on 15 December. Unfortunately, the first attempt to execute him failed, as the rope broke. The sympathetic crowd urged him to escape, but MacNaughten refused, remounting the gallows with the now famous words that he would rather die than be known 'as Half-hanged MacNaughten for the rest of his life'. He waited patiently on the gallows while another rope was found. The rope did not break a second time. After his death, MacNaughton was decapitated. His body lies in the graveyard of Strabane Church, County Tyrone.

ON 26 March 2004, sportsman Jimmy Payne, of Waterford City, smashed the existing solo 24-hour skipping record of 130,000 skips when he skipped an amazing 141,221 skips in a 24-hour period. In front of a huge crowd at the City Square Shopping Centre, Payne – a holder of four national boxing titles – skipped an average 175–180 skips per minute, using the record attempt to raise more than €26,000 for Our Lady's Hospital for Sick Children. Far from being new to record-breaking, Jimmy Payne was the leader of the team that set the 24-hour team skipping record of 244,949 skips in 2002.

IN 1781, a relative of the famous writer Dorothea Herbert, Mrs Cooke of Clontarf, Dublin, became unhinged with grief after the death of her beloved husband. In her *Retrospections*, Herbert recounts the beautiful young widow's strange behaviour. After several weeks in solitary seclusion, Mrs Cooke emerged from her bedroom and announced her plans to put her entire house in mourning for her late husband. She took to dressing in black and directed her servants and two young daughters to do likewise. She ordered every inch of the house's woodwork painted black – even down to the stable doors and hay mangers. A visitor who put his horse in the stables while the paint was still wet was amused by the results. 'It happened to be a white one,' Dorothea Herbert wrote, 'and having well rubbed its snowy hide it was led out to its master an elegant piebald.' He was furious and caned the stable boy at length 'for his impertinence' until Mrs Cooke intervened and explained that the stables were freshly painted black. Even flowerpots were painted black to pacify the disturbed widow. Not content with these changes, Mrs Cooke invited an upholsterer to make further radical alterations to complete her household makeover. Herbert has left us a wonderful description of the encounter: 'He was shown at midday into a large dark room where the fair widow sat (with a taper burning) in deepest woe and dress'd in her sables – she arose at his entrance, received him graciously but silently, and after sitting some time weeping she told the poor wonder-stricken upholsterer that she had a job for him which she expected he would perform with all privacy and fidelity – she showed him every hole and corner of the house – bespoke hangings of black paper for every room – black beds, black chair-covers, black window curtains.' The poor man listened in silent horror and she detailed her ambitions to 'blacken' everything in the house. When she commanded her maid Betty – also dressed in black – to lock him in a room until he agreed to do the work, the upholsterer escaped after giving 'one spring from the top of the stairs to the bottom'. Eventually the widow was cured of her melancholy feelings and the house and household returned to colour, but she never remarried.

~

IRISHMAN Sergeant Michael Connelley was in charge of the soldiers' hospital in Salamanca in Spain during the Peninsular War against Napoleon. He drank 'like a whale' and died of alcoholic poisoning shortly after the battle of Salamanca in July 1812. He was very attentive to the sick, but was best known for his eccentric concern that the British would die well in the face of the French wounded. One eyewitness quotes Connelley's bedside manner: 'Merciful God! What more do you want? You'll be buried in a shroud and coffin, won't you? For God's sake, die like a man before these 'ere Frenchers.' Sergeant Connelley was very popular through the Army and a great many soldiers attended his funeral. One of the pallbearers, a cockney ventriloquist, knocked on the coffin and imitated Connelley's voice. 'Oh, merciful Jesus, I'm smothered.' The cortège stopped, bayonets were produced, and the lid prised off to reveal the still dead sergeant. At the time the incident was thought to be extremely funny and in good taste, which says a lot for the gallow's humour of soldiers at war.

~

DUBLINER John Nicholson (1821–57) was one of the legendary figures of British India. As a soldier-administrator, he was without equal. He had the rare gift of winning absolute trust and devotion from the native people among whom he worked in the subcontinent. Nicholson was held in such high regard that, at the age of 27, one group decided that he was a reincarnation of Brahma and deified him as 'Nikal Seyn'. They worshiped Nicholson with a fervour that greatly annoyed him. He even went so far as to have some of his worshippers imprisoned and whipped (none of which shook the steadfastness of their devotion!). In spite of Nicholson's efforts, the cult flourished, and when he fell at the Siege of Delhi, during the Indian Mutiny, several devotees committed suicide, while the rest converted to Christianity, declaring: 'Nikal Seyn always said that he was a man such as we are, and that he worshipped a God we could not see but who was always near us. Let us then learn to worship Nikal Seyn's God.'

AMAZINGLY, bagpipes do not feature on the musical score of Mel Gibson's film *Braveheart*. The reason why the haunting music features Irish Uilleann pipes rather than the more appropriate Scottish bagpipes is explained by Mel Gibson on his director's commentary on the *Braveheart* DVD: 'The Uillieann pipes were just more melodic because the Scottish bagpipes tend to sound like a scalded cat. I just found the Irish pipes to be more romantic.' *Braveheart* tells the story of William Wallace (c. 1270–1305), a Scottish patriot who led a campaign against English occupation of Scotland. Uillieann pipes were invented at the beginning of the 18th century.

IN February 1930 this peculiar-shaped egg was laid by a hen belonging to Mrs Balding of Ballyshannon, County Carlow.

⁊

GEORGE THOMAS (1756–1802) from Roscrea, County Tipperary went to India in the late 18th century and became a mercenary for hire, drilling and training native troops in the superior method of European warfare.

Tiring of the duplicitous and miserly ways of his Indian employers, Thomas struck out on his own. With his faithful followers, the Irish warlord headed for a vulnerable no man's land in the most fertile part of India, west of Delhi. Through a mixture of the military genius and extreme violence for which he was famous, Thomas carved out a large kingdom for himself and proved to be a benevolent ruler whose subjects prospered under his rule. The Irish Rajah was a progressive leader, rebuilding towns, re-establishing the rule of law, encouraging settlers in a previously sparsely uninhabited and war-torn countryside. He instituted pensions for his troops – something unheard of at that time – and even minted his own coins. To fund his state, Thomas hired out his army and military genius to neighbouring states for hard cash. His unbroken string of victories made Thomas a threat to rival military powers. They were so envious of his meteoric rise to power that they did the unthinkable – they joined together. Thomas had other plans and was determined to fight to the last. At one stage his 2,000 men fought and won an epic battle against 40,000 troops. Thomas's fame spread across continents. Wellington even studied his military campaigns and adopted his tactics. Now he is all but forgotten, except for the descendants of his subjects, who still remember him as a legendary hero. At the end of his life he agreed to dictate his autobiography in Persian, 'as from constant use it was more familiar than his native language'. It is no wonder that Thomas may have inspired Kipling's story 'The Man Who Would Be King', which was later turned into a film starring Sean Connery and Michael Caine.

∽

LOUGH Neagh is the largest lake in Britain or Ireland. It is located in five of the six counties of Northern Ireland: Tyrone, Derry, Down, Antrim and Armagh. Fermanagh is the exception.

∽

DURING the siege by Cromwellian troops of Clonmel in 1650, one attack was led by a Colonel Charles Langley. As he tried to climb over the defences, his hand was cut off by a scythe. He survived and was granted lands at Ballinagarry, County Tipperary. He later had a steel replacement hand made and the hand is said to have remained in the family until the early 20th century.

∽

IN 1903, Dublin Corporation built Ireland's first major power plant (3 mega watts) at Pigeon House. The remote location was once ridiculed, but electricity is still generated there a century later at the Poolbeg power station (900 mega watts). Pigeon House was the first station in the world to generate three-phase electricity – basically using a more efficient generator with three wire coils instead of one – and it was a model for other stations around the world.

⤔

GEORGE BARRINGTON (1755–1810) was a notorious gentleman pickpocket from Maynooth, County Kildare whose eloquence in the dock astonished judge and jurors alike. His silver tongue saved his life and he was transported to Botany Bay in Australia for his daring crimes, where he turned over a new leaf. He later became one of its most respected citizens and was police chief of the town of Parramatta near Sydney for a considerable period.

⤔

BEAUTIFUL but violent Lola Montez (1820–61) from County Sligo left a trail of lovers, spent fortunes and caused scandals in her adventures around the world. In her time she was probably the most outrageous woman in the world. She caused a king (Ludwig I of Bavaria) to lose his throne, set off rebellions and riots and mesmerised men. Ex-lover Alexandre Dumas said, 'She is fatal to any man who dares love her.'

⤔

AT 62 metres high, the Wellington Monument looms over the skyline of Dublin's Phoenix Park. It is the largest obelisk in Europe. The brass panels on its plinth were cast from captured French cannon and depict scenes from the Duke of Wellington's war victories in India and at Waterloo.

✍

A letter once took 38 years (1872–1910) to get from Dublin to Pomeroy, County Tyrone – and back! The letter contained a circular from Mr David Drimmie, the then Resident Secretary of the English and Scottish Law Life Assurance Association, to one of his agents. After a lapse of 38 years it returned to one of Mr Drimmie's sons, who filled the position formerly held by his father at the same address. No explanation was ever given by the post office authorities for the delay, although someone must have some knowledge of the long-concealed whereabouts of the letter and the manner of its discovery. The envelope was simply marked: 'Not known at Pomeroy'.

✍

AFTER the death of Peter Warren Locke in 1832, Athgoe Park, Hazelhatch, County Dublin passed to his two sisters, Mrs Skerrett and Mrs O'Carroll. Some years later, Mrs O'Carroll's son, Redmond O'Carroll, was looking through a bundle of old leases when a paper fell out which he discovered was the will of Peter Warren Locke, leaving all his estates and property to his illegiti-mate daughter. Being an honourable man, O'Carroll did not destroy the document as others might have done. He promptly handed it over to Locke's daughter – even though that meant the O'Carrolls and the Skerretts would now lose their inheritance. Eventually the property passed to Redmond's nephew, F.J.L. O'Carroll.

IN September 1998, an Irish drug smuggler was caught after reporting his suitcase (containing 16 kilos of cannabis) was missing. Christopher Dowling, 20, a burglar alarm engineer from County Kildare, took a flight from Dublin to Cardiff. Unknown to him, his luggage took a different flight. When he got to Cardiff, his suitcase was nowhere to be seen on the airport baggage carousel. Dowling reported it missing and checked into a local bed and breakfast while he waited for it to turn up. The bag was eventually traced to Teeside Airport, where customs officers opened it to confirm ownership and discovered the cannabis. Dowling was arrested by customs officials when he went to pick it up from the airport the next day, and was later sentenced to two years' imprisonment.

TUCKEY'S *Cork Remembrancer* (1837) records the death of a 'poor labouring' man from Ovens, County Cork in the early 19th century who died at the age of 127. 'He walked four months before he died without the help of a stick or crutch, could see without spectacles, retained his senses and appetite to the last, and was followed to the grave by his descendants to the seventh generation.'

IN January 1990, fate played a cruel trick on a rare American bittern which survived an epic flight across the Atlantic to County Wexford, only to killed by a dog. The heron-like bird was believed to be the first of its type to be recorded in Britain or Ireland for eight years, and only the ninth in 30 years.

❧

IN the London *Journal of Cutaneous Medicine* (1868, vol. 2), Dr Purdon recounted the strange case of a 40-year-old Irish woman, suffering from rheumatic fever. What was unusual about this patient is that occasionally a blue discharge or sweat literally flowed from her legs and body. The patient denied taking any coloured substance or chemical that might have affected the colour of her perspiration.

❧

ON 12 March 1978 the Dublin Welsh Male Voice Choir managed to come second in a choral contest – despite being the only entrants. The choir had entered in two sections of a competition that took place in Arklow, County Wicklow. They planned to sing 'Roman War Song' from Wagner's opera *Rienzi* in the open section and a medley of Welsh hymns in the sacred music section. On arrival in the town, the choir went to the Arklow Bay Hotel, where they had allegedly reserved rehearsal facilities. Finding another choir using their rooms, the Dublin Welsh males adjourned to the bar until the rooms became available. Later, a stern-faced contest organiser burst into the rehearsal rooms as the choir was running through a few pieces and angrily told them they were late. They raced up, bounded on to the stage and prepared to give the performance of their lives. Unfortunately, their conductor did not know which section this was and never bothered to ask. Under his able direction, the choir launched into a rendition of the 'Roman War Song'. Only after they had finished did they realise that they were performing in the sacred music section. The adjudicator was forgiving and made favourable remarks on what was a well-sung, though highly inappropriate, piece. The choir had been the only entry in this section, and it seemed to all that they would (naturally) win it! The authorities displayed great unease at the prospect of awarding first prize to this irresponsible lot. Instead, they awarded them second, which was a cheque for £40 and no cup. First prize had been a cup and £80. During the week one of the choir related the bizarre story to a journalist friend. The journalist rang the contest organisers in Arklow to confirm that the only entry in a competition had come second. The organisers asked 'what are they complaining about?' The story later featured in the *Daily Mirror*, who gave the choir £50 for their story. Including the *Daily Mirror* money, the Dublin Welsh Male Voice Choir had managed to come out ahead, despite being second in what was a one-horse race.

IN July 2006 a 16-month-old female cat called Salem displayed its homing ability when she trekked 50 miles back to her old home after having been given away to a new home. The emaciated cat could barely raise a feeble 'meow' when she arrived at the back door of the

Heneghan family's farmhouse near Partry, County Mayo 13 days after she had been given away as a present to friends living near Gurteen, County Sligo. Her owner, Kathleen Heneghan, says that Salem had disappeared immediately after being taken out of her cardboard box and introduced to her new owners.